The
Church

Brent D.
Peterson

THE FOUNDRY
PUBLISHING°

The Foundry Publishing®
PO Box 419527
Kansas City, MO 64141
thefoundrypublishing.com

978-0-8341-4224-4

Printed in the
United States of America

Cover design: Arthur Cherry
Interior design: Sharon Page

Library of Congress Cataloging-in-Publication Data
A complete catalog record for this book is available from the Library of Congress.

The internet addresses, email addresses, and phone numbers in this book are accurate at the time of publication. They are provided as a resource. The Foundry Publishing® does not endorse them or vouch for their content or permanence.

10 9 8 7 6 5 4 3 2 1

This book is dedicated to three pastoral couples who,
in addition to my family, embodied a deep love of
Jesus in the church as the body of Christ:
Tharon and Barbara Daniels
Ron and Kay Lush
Jesse and Susan Middendorf

Contents

XI. The Church

We believe in the church, the community that confesses Jesus Christ as Lord, the covenant people of God made new in Christ, the body of Christ called together by the Holy Spirit through the Word.

God calls the church to express its life in the unity and fellowship of the Spirit; in worship through the preaching of the Word, observance of the sacraments, and ministry in his name; by obedience to Christ, holy living, and mutual accountability.

The mission of the church in the world is to share in the redemptive and reconciling ministry of Christ in the power of the Spirit. The church fulfills its mission by making disciples through evangelism, education, showing compassion, working for justice, and bearing witness to the kingdom of God.

The church is a historical reality that organizes itself in culturally conditioned forms, exists both as local congregations and as a universal body, and also sets apart persons called of God for specific ministries. God calls the church to live under his rule in anticipation of the consummation at the coming of our Lord Jesus Christ.[1]

---

1. Church of the Nazarene, "Articles of Faith: XI. The Church," Church Constitution, *Manual: 2017–2021* (Kansas City, MO: Nazarene Publishing House, 2017), 33.

Introduction

Is the church on its deathbed? Some may expect a book on the church either to be a historical account about what *was*, or a bell tolling the impending death of the church. Curiously, those who are ready to write the coroner's report for the church are often white, U.S.-centric, middle-class, self-proclaimed experts who fail to consider how the church is thriving around the globe and even in the United States among nonwhite congregations.[1] While the decline in worship attendance in white churches, along with the rise of what we call the "nones" (those who do not claim any religious affiliation), is worthy of reflection, it is important also to acknowledge that God continues to provide new life in places we often miss.

As God keeps calling the church to deeper levels of faithfulness, certain practices and imaginations of the church need to be put to death in order that resurrection life may flourish. The church must seek to better reflect the image of Jesus—born in poverty in an occupied land, among the civically and religiously marginalized, crucified and resurrected. Too often Christians seek to enjoy the gifts of Christ without wanting to follow and *become like* Christ. This error has produced people who are *fans* of Jesus but resist being *followers*. Rather than a Savior who seeks

---

1. See Soong-Chan Rah, *The Next Evangelicalism: Freeing the Church from West-ern Cultural Captivity* (Downers Grove, IL: InterVarsity Press, 2009).

to transform our lives, some Christians imagine Jesus as a benevolent superhero.

I have always loved Superman. From the Saturday-morning cartoon *Super Friends* to the Christopher Reeve movies, Superman was my favorite hero. He was faster and stronger than everyone else and thus easy to cheer for (just watch out for that kryptonite!). Yet Superman does not have any real partners. In the movies, he battles General Zod or the evil genius Lex Luthor on his own. Superman handles his business. He does not need any help, and the key is to not get in his way. Since I can't really relate to Superman, he invites me to be a *fan*, and that is fun and does not cost me anything.

Without care, Christians may begin to treat Jesus as simply a fun superhero. Jesus does cool stuff for us, we are thankful, and our job is to not get in the way. Being a fan of Jesus costs us nothing. Yet Jesus does not seek to have *fans* but *followers* whose lives will reflect him. Jesus did not say, "Look at me as I take up my cross to secure your salvation." Jesus did not say, "Look at me as I die for your sins and then am raised." Jesus invites all to be disciples: "All who want to come after me must say no to themselves, take up their cross, and follow me. All who want to save their lives will lose them. But all who lose their lives because of me will find them" (Matthew 16:24b–25). While following Jesus is the road to life, following that narrow road requires discipline and focus (see Matthew 7:13–14).

So do you want to be a *fan* or a *follower* of Jesus? This book explores what it means to be followers (or disciples) of Jesus as his body in the martyr church. Paul's metaphor for the church as the body of Christ has become a primary symbol that continues to offer imagination and wonder (see 1 Corinthians 12). In faithfully being and becoming the body of Christ, the church by the power of the Spirit is invited to continually mature and be healed into the image of Christ.

At its core, the church is united with the body of the crucified and resurrected Christ—this is *martyr ecclesiology.* In order to contrast a martyr ecclesiology from what I call *empire ecclesiology,* this text will journey with Christ in the Gospels and consider how this revelation of Christ shapes the church in its work participating in God's mission in the world. We will explore martyr ecclesiology through a Wesleyan lens.

Wesleyan Ecclesial Confession

John and Charles Wesley came from a parsonage home that was passionately devoted to God in eighteenth-century England. During their studies at Oxford, their zeal and devotion for God grew and matured. They became deeply distressed by many they encountered who were happy to speak about an admiration and appreciation for Jesus Christ but who did not reflect Christ's love in their lives. The Wesleys felt they were saturated in a culture of casual Christians, where individuals were *fans* of Jesus and of God's forgiveness of their own sins but were not actively *following* and being *transformed* by Christ. Their pastoral tone was not one of harsh judgment and condemnation for those Christians but one of gracious invitation for people to become devoted *followers.*

The Wesley brothers were convinced that God desired to offer more than forgiveness as a get-out-of-hell card. Forgiveness was about a healing relationship of growing and maturing in holy love. This maturing in love was embodied by a vigorous rhythm of communal worship and missional engagement in one's community. Being transformed by holy love is a kind of healing that empowers care for the hurting and oppressed—where one would find God already present and at work. In this way, the martyr church is present to persons and to God in holy love and compassion. The Wesleys had their struggles and did not always get it right, but their strong commitment to what I call the martyr church will be a primary theme that frames this conversation. This Wesleyan passion is mostly in harmony with Orthodox, Roman Catholic, Lutheran, Reformed, Baptist, nondenominational, and other traditions. However, a Wesleyan rhythm and tune will be uniquely highlighted along the way. Those specific places will be noted as a *Wesleyan Ecclesial Confession.*

This exploration of the martyr church as the body of the crucified and resurrected Christ will be woven through three interconnected sections. Section 1 begins with God— where, out of the triune dance of love, God creates in order that *love might flourish.*[2] God creates humans out of a passion that creatures can receive, share, and participate in God's love. The God who created in *kenotic* (self-emptying) love also sends the Son to become incarnate in Jesus Christ in order that humanity, as part of creation, could find healing from sin and maturity in love. The conversation also journeys with the disciples who were trying to find their way from the fishing ship into disciple-ship. Section 1 concludes with the blessing of the Spirit. At Pentecost the Holy Spirit was poured out, birthing and empowering the church, inviting all to discipleship.

Section 2 begins by celebrating God's call upon all humans as ministers of the gospel in their work in the world. Among these believers God also calls humans for leadership in the church. This section also considers the gift of a covenantal polity (church organization) that seeks to guide the church in its ministry within and outside the body. After attending to good practices in church leadership

---

2. This phrase was first gifted to me by my professor and friend Michael Lodahl.

and the importance of navigating conflict well, this section concludes by giving attention to those who have been wounded by the church.

Section 3 explores the great gift and calling of the church to participate in God's mission in the world. Within this mission there is caution against the allure of empire and the temptation toward dualism. The martyr church is to live as those who celebrate the further inbreaking of the kingdom coming to earth, resisting an empire imagination that seeks purpose through dominance and exploitation. As part of the coming of the new creation, the martyr church works toward justice for the healing of *all* the nations in a spirit of generous hospitality. In a hospitality of compassion, as one encounters the oppressed and marginalized, God and the martyr church are found.

Any conversation on the church must attend to the primary work the church has been called to do: communal worship. Suggesting that communal worship is the primary *liturgy* ("work of the people") of the church does not discount all the important aspects of evangelism, discipleship, and missional work for justice in the world. This rhythm of God breathing into Christians for communal worship and exhaling them out for mission is central to the healthy life of the church. The communal worship gathering and the gifts of preaching and the sacraments will be addressed in detail in the *Sacraments* volume of *The Wesleyan Theology Series*.

In every introductory book, each subject raised deserves deeper engagement. As such, many (including the author) may be frustrated that this book is a mile wide but an inch deep. My prayer is that this conversation helps readers fall in love more deeply with the church—universal and local—as the present reflection of the body of the crucified and resurrected Jesus Christ. In the spirit of Philippians 1:16, the God who birthed and empowered the church will continue to help it move more fully toward maturity in love. Confidence in God provides great hope that the church can more fully be and become the body of the crucified and resurrected Christ. Only as the church allows itself to take up its cross and die with Christ can it enter into resurrection life.

The Essence of the Church

The essence of the church begins and ends with the triune God. Moreover, the church is simply part of the gift of God's creation, infused with divine purpose and calling. As creation bursts forth with the hope and design that God's love might flourish, within God's providence the invitation to love does not force a receptive response. Despite the invitation and calling to love, humanity chose away from God's love. Yet God did not leave humanity and creation enslaved to death and sin but continues to work toward our healing and redemption.

15

As part of God's continual work of new creation and redemption, the Father sends the Son by the power of the Spirit. In the life, death, and resurrection of Jesus, the triune God works to redeem all of creation. The method of this redemption is not one of empire that seeks to control by violence and domination. Instead, the cruciform power of the crucified God becomes the model and means for the church, which is fully birthed by the sending of the Spirit. In this way the people of God are formed into the body of the crucified and resurrected Christ as the martyr church that resists the seduction of liturgies and imaginations of empire.

> This section thus begins by considering the hope of the martyr church that participates in God's work to redeem all creation.

ONE

The Hope of the Martyr Church

What does it mean to be the body of the crucified and resurrected Christ? Without any desire to be condescending or patronizing, too often it feels like Christians have lost Christ as the one they follow. When any hoard food, shelter, and clothing while others go without, Christ has been forgotten (see Luke 12:13–21). Christ is disregarded when any person is exploited or oppressed or devalued based on any number of demographic, social, or other identifying details. Christ is abandoned when my own comfort and tranquility come by way of the suffering of another. Christ is lost when my physical survival is the ultimate goal that justifies all other actions.

As a means of confession and repentance, this conversation seeks to prophetically imagine how the church can better follow and reflect the image of Jesus—who embodied love and was crucified for doing so. This book will explore two ways of living that serve as foils on the same continuum. On one end is the seduction of the empire church; the other is the invitation to the martyr church. The empire church and martyr church are not binary choices. We are not *either* one *or* the other. Rather, what actions, attitudes, and postures move us closer to one and further from the other?

The Seduction of Empire

In its extreme form, the way of empire is rooted in fear and encourages us to seek our own happiness at the expense of those around us. The way of empire tells us we should take matters into our own hands, refusing to trust anyone else because other people are potential threats. We embody the way of empire when we only offer care and hospitality to people who look, act, and/or think like we do.

Within an empire imagination, our personal liberties and freedoms must never be transgressed—even if that means other humans will suffer. Economic and political violence are tools wielded to eliminate real or perceived threats to our way of life. We offer allegiance to empire as the primary source of hope and security even at the expense of creaturely collateral damage. The way of empire is first about ourselves; other persons are often objectified for our personal gain. The way of empire is ultimately anxious and insecure—never at rest or peace, for fear others are ready to take what we believe is ours.

The seduction of empire is this and much more. One danger of framing empire in that way is that it can be rather abstract and easily repulsive. In real life, very few people *set out* to be the evil, maniacal mastermind bent on destroying everyone's life through empire. Yet seduction rarely presents itself as the destructive force it actually is. Empire embraces banal subtlety as its corrosive cancer slowly spreads.

Invitation into the Martyr Church

While most are repulsed by empire as it's just been described, the idea of and the term "martyr" may also seem unappealing. What does it mean to be the martyr church?

As I lead U.S. Christian students into this idea, I often receive puzzled looks. My students often have both negative and positive images of martyrdom. Negatively, some quickly think of a suicide bomber in a crowded market, trying to kill as many people as possible in the name of some ideology or faith. Some imagine a martyr as someone who seeks death for the sake of glory in this life and/or some reward in the next. Positively, students often celebrate those who have been persecuted and have died for their faith. Curiously, students often think positively about martyrdom when it is associated with their own faith and negatively when it describes other faiths. Sadly, they often imagine persons of other world faiths principally as terrorists who do violent action, but these same students are often slow to categorize as terrorism violent acts done by those who share their own nationality and religion. Later we will further clarify that a Christian martyr never seeks death but rather lays down one's life for the sake of the other as an act of love.

Often my students admit that both the positive and negative images of martyrdom seem irrelevant to their U.S. American Christian context. Craig Hovey explores martyrdom in *To Share in the Body* precisely for a church that feels the idea is either only negative or irrelevant when we presume an entire nation is "Christian." Succinctly, to be a martyr means to suffer, be persecuted, often be killed, for the simple act of bearing witness to one's faith or beliefs. Hovey says, "Martyrdom is not a witness gone terribly wrong but the ultimate paradigm of witness."[1] Too often among U.S. American Christians, preserving life is the ultimate goal, even if that may hamper our witness to Christ.

To be part of the martyr church is to not settle for being a *fan*, or admirer, of Jesus but to be a disciple, a *follower*, one who will pick up her cross and follow Christ—come what may. Some important aspects to highlight about martyrdom include:

---

1. Craig Hovey, *To Share in the Body: A Theology of Martyrdom for Today's Church* (Grand Rapids: Brazos Press, 2008), 18.

1) Martyrdom is not *seeking* or *desiring* to die. The early church challenged the cult of martyrs who sought the glory of being killed. Seeking to die is suicide, not martyrdom.

2) While persons in the martyr church do not seek death, they are willing to be faithful even as death may come.

3) Martyrdom is always a result of witness. It is not a strategy and not a good in and of itself. "There is *no reason* for disciples to die, in that they will accomplish anything by their deaths. But this is not sufficient to keep them from becoming martyrs, since . . . martyrs do not die for 'reasons.'"[2] Hovey says that if we supply a good reason, strategy, or purpose for why we may be able to die, we may find a reason to escape it.[3]

4) Martyrdom is not focused on individual death but on finding life by being immersed in the death and resurrection of Jesus.

5) Martyrdom is a gift. "It is better to speak of martyrdom as itself a gift and not a way of accomplishing something. Martyrs do not die in order to make a point. They do not mean to show the courage of the Christian, the wickedness of the world, the integrity and truth of Christian beliefs . . . or even the fact that God can be trusted. . . . The only thing they mean is the meaning their lives and deaths are given to God."[4]

The martyr church invites persons to discipleship in Jesus Christ, taking up their cross by the power of the Spirit.

---

2. Hovey, *To Share in the Body*, 93.
3. Hovey, *To Share in the Body*, 108.
4. Hovey, *To Share in the Body*, 143.

The Martyr Church for Victims

When we discuss the invitation to the martyr church, one group in particular needs special attention. Jesus Christ came to earth and intentionally entered into the pain and despair of many who have been sinned against. The church has often failed to pay attention pastorally and theologically to the victims of sin. For victims, the road to salvation includes the restoration of a healthy ego and self-esteem. Many who have been victimized find salvation in properly loving and caring for themselves in their journey of healing.

Inviting victims to join the martyr church may be understood as telling persons to remain in abuse and continue to be a doormat to the powerful oppressor. This is certainly not what the martyr church is about! For many Christians, the journey into the martyr church is not serving others from a place of brokenness but taking time to find appropriate and necessary healing from past abuse and trauma. Only when someone experiences and understands their worth and value in God's love will they be ready to offer themselves to love and serve others in thanksgiving.

Martyr Vs. Empire

In considering the seduction of empire and the invitation of the martyr church, I am concerned that such distinctions not be reduced to sentimental abstractions from how we live each day. Our daily activities and practices (liturgies) shape our imagination, and form us toward citizenship either in the martyr church or the empire. This discussion is not about pious sentimentalities that simply inspire cognitive assent. While the rest of the book will explore this continuum, below are a few ways to frame the distinctions.

Martyr Church	Empire Church
Life given back to God in doxology	Life centered on personal/individual happiness
Find joy in serving	Others should serve me
Set free from the fear of death	Ready to use violence to prevent my own death
All humans valued as created in God's image	Others who are not like me are devalued and worthy of suspicion
Love enemies	Conquer and/or kill enemies
God's kingdom in all nations	My nation is the center of God's kingdom
Abundance of grace	Myth of scarcity

May we have the courage to repent of our tendencies toward empire and draw upon the Spirit to courageously pick up our cross and follow Christ as the martyr church.

TWO | The Triune Dance of Love

All Christian stories begin and end in God. The beautiful hymn of Genesis 1 celebrates the God who creates—where life, light, and beauty explode forth into existence. Where there had been emptiness and darkness, without form and shape, deserted and void of life, God speaks forth the brilliance of all creation (see Genesis 1:1–3; 27; 2:20–23). In a devastating distortion of the gospel, some Christians reduce its message to an individual, hedonistic aim that is only concerned with "getting to heaven." This reduction undermines the very humanity into which we are formed, deeply entangled with one another and this natural world, in responsibility. If individual salvation is extracted from the story of creation, ecclesiology is an unimportant theological addendum. What is lost, however, is both our own humanity and the God whose love and presence are best known to the Good Samaritan (see Luke 10:35–37).

To understand how the work of Jesus relates to our bodies and relationships, we will reach back to the very beginning, to the song of creation—a celebration of God's creation of the world as an expression of love that includes plants, animals, and humans created in the image of God to love and be loved. Before this exploration, grounding all theological discourse as prayer becomes essential.

Theology as Prayer

Christian theology is best understood as a prayer of thanksgiving in response to God's revelation of love. As prayer, the goal of theology is not trying to exhaust God's mystery but to be transformed by God, becoming more fully human. Similarly, the encounter is not simply *about* God but *with* God and, as such, inviting transformation.

This divine-human encounter with God is the foundation for how we are to properly consider who the church *is* and is to *become*. The revelation of the triune God illuminates the full hope of humanity and, as such, the hope of the church—the body of the crucified and resurrected Jesus Christ.

Theology, as a mode of prayer, leans us into the mystery of the triune God not principally for logical answers but for transformation in holy love.

The Triune God: A Doxological Mystery

Conversations on the Trinity are best understood as a type of prayer that is *paradoxical*. A paradox is often considered in places where there is an apparent contradiction. As a paradox, the glory of God is beyond human comprehension, but it certainly invites us to be encountered by God in order to be more fully transformed in a *kenotic* (self-giving) love that seeks to empower, encourage, and uplift the other.

One of the primary tenets of later Judaism is its strident monotheism (one deity) that specifically rejects polytheism (multiple deities). Yahweh alone is God. Yet were these Jews, who were followers of Jesus Christ, to worship him as God? Was the second Person of the Trinity, incarnate as Jesus, *created* or *eternal*? The councils of Nicaea in 325, Constantinople in 381, and Chalcedon in 451 celebrate Christ as truly God and truly human. It became *orthodox* (right worship, more than simply belief) to confess that the Son shares the same essence as the Father and is eternal. Along with affirming the divinity of the Spirit, the church would come to worship God as one-in-three and three-in-one.[1] The Athanasian Creed confesses: "For there is one person of the Father, another of the Son, and another of the Holy Spirit. But the Godhead of the Father, of the Son, and of the Holy Spirit is all one, the glory equal, the majesty coeternal. Such as the Father is, such is the Son, and such is the Holy Spirit."[2] So what does this affirmation of the triune God have to do with a martyr ecclesiology?

Kenotic and Cruciform Love

First, since God is both one and three, within God there is a giving and receiving of love. There is a lover and a beloved, a beautiful dance of love that is often described as the divine *perichoresis*. This love is not one of hierarchy, competition, or objectification; instead, it is a love of empowerment and mutual celebration. Moreover, as revealed and embodied in the triune movement in Jesus Christ, this love is both *kenotic* and *cruciform*.

As *kenotic*, it seeks in humility to serve the other out of love and devotion. In Jesus Christ, the very understanding of God's power is embodied in becoming truly human— the incarnation. God in Christ became human, with all humanity's frailty and sinfulness, in order to redeem and restore humanity. The opposite of *kenotic* love would be to live in a hierarchical economy where the goal is to dominate, exploit, and objectify others for personal gain. Those with the biggest sword and the largest throne demand praise, honor, and service from those below them, who are

---

1. For a more detailed treatment of the doctrine of the Trinity, see Samuel M. Powell, *The Wesleyan Theological Series: The Trinity* (Kansas City, MO: The Foundry Publishing, 2020).

2. "Athanasian Creed," Christian Classics Ethereal Library, https://www.ccel.org/creeds/athanasian.creed.html, lines 5–7.

imagined as worth less (or worthless). A failure to serve the powerful leaves the weak open to violence. Fear is the primary liturgy in this empire imagination for both oppressor and oppressed.

On the other hand, as an extension of *kenotic* love, the triune God embodies *cruciform* love poured out upon creation. A cruciform love enters into the pain and despair of the created order so creation may be healed and redeemed through a reconciliation of love. The temptation of empire is to find meaning through control, domination, and exploitation. Conversely, living into a martyr imagination finds life through service, care, and generous hospitality.

Genesis 1:27 celebrates that humans are created in God's image. We know from the testimony of Jesus that to live into the gift of being created in God's image is to love God, self, and neighbor as an act of joyful thanksgiving (see Matthew 22:37–40). These loves can never be disentangled. Too often Christians try to separate these loves, creating an unfortunate imbalance between love of God, neighbor, and self. From Genesis to Revelation Scripture is clear that we love God *by* loving neighbor, the other, and specifically those who may consider us their enemy.

I can't love God and hate Eric. This simply will not work. Rather, my love of God flourishes in my love for Eric and Eric's love for me. Christian cruciform love is not convenient or comfortable. Eric is bound to me and I to Eric in a love that embraces the joy and suffering of others (see Romans 12:15). This love is *kenotic* as we give ourselves for the sake of the other—not as denying ourselves but as properly loving ourselves. While all love begins first as a gift from God, we receive this love of God most often first through humans loving us. Hence, our love for God is properly known through our love for others and a healthy love for self (see Matthew 25:31–46).

The Sin of Subjugation

In the Wesleyan tradition God's *kenotic* love empowers, invites, and woos—but does not coerce. Humans are invited to respond to God's love by loving other humans and the rest of creation. Sadly, humans have not always responded well in this creation hymn to the invitation to love. Failure to love is sin. Sin is a failure to love other humans, ourselves, and God. Sin moves us away from life and love and toward death and nothingness. From the garden forward, it becomes clear that the choice to sin is devastating to all creation. The apostle Paul notes the cosmic pain as a result of sin: "We know that the whole creation is groaning together and suffering labor pains up until now" (Romans 8:22). This failure to love demonstrates creation's immaturity and the need for God's continual power and presence to offer healing and maturity in love.

As the story of Genesis unfolds, one of the results of the fall into sin is the rise of humans dominating and subjugating other humans in exploitation and oppression. More will be said about this later in regard to church leadership, but it must be clearly understood that *all people* are equally created in God's image.[3] If we affirm that all people, not just some, are created in the image of God, there are tremendous implications for how we imagine both God and the church. Along with Paul, we celebrate that part of God's healing of sin in the world is to renew all things, now and into the future. This renewal is a restoration of the blessed equality (not "sameness") of all people: "There is neither Jew nor Greek; there is neither slave nor free; nor is there male and female, for you are all one in Christ Jesus" (Galatians 3:28). Twenty-first-century ears must be

---

3. Chapter 7 celebrates the long-held Wesleyan affirmation that God calls, equips, empowers, and desires both women *and* men to hold all leadership positions in the church.

careful not to miss the radicality of Paul's declaration about equality. Sadly, the church has been a primary place where persons have experienced discrimination based on demographic differences.

At its core, the gospel celebrates the God who created out of love but did not abandon humanity when humanity failed to love well. Instead, God offered and still offers forgiveness, healing, and new life. Yet this healing and forgiveness are costly because they come through God's *cruciform* love—God's choice to lay down God's own life for the healing of creation. God keeps offering new life to those who have chosen death. God has not given up and will not give up on creation. The church abides in this confident hope. The goal and hope for the full healing of creation is the renewal of all things to more fully participate in the triune dance of love. In that beautiful prayer in John 17, Christ prays, "I pray they will be one, Father, just as you are in me and I am in you. I pray that they also will be in us, so that the world will believe that you sent me. I've given them the glory that you gave me so that they can be one just as we are one. I'm in them and you are in me so that they will be made perfectly one. Then the world will know that you sent me and that you have loved them just as you loved me" (vv. 21–23).

From the beginning, God creates so that humans would love and be loved well by humans as they also lovingly care and nurture the rest of the created order. God's love flourishing in creation is precisely how God is glorified and will "be all in all" (1 Corinthians 15:28). God's *kenotic* and cruciform love becomes the air into which a martyr ecclesiology is birthed and sustained.

THREE

God Became Flesh

Because God refuses to give up on humanity even when humanity chooses sin, God continues to woo and invite humans to find healing and to move from sin toward love. The Wesleyan tradition affirms the idea of prevenient grace, meaning God always makes the first move in love, then invites humanity to respond. Since God is the primary actor in the ongoing healing of creation, God invites and empowers humans to participate with God in the healing and redemptive mission God is working in the world.

After the challenging Noah narrative and the disappointment of humanity's pursuit of selfish aims with the Tower of Babel, God reached out to a barren, nomadic couple, through whom God desired to spread the message of hope in Yahweh and also through whom God intended for all nations to be blessed (see Genesis 12:1–3). God does love all people but specifically chose to covenant with a particular group of people whose mission was to reflect the image of God outward in order that hope and redemption may grow and expand in the world.

This calling to be God's unique people comes with the responsibility of seeing God's love flourish in creation. Abraham and Sarah and their descendants had moments when they faithfully reflected God's image, but they also had many moments of failing to live into this calling. Too often God's people embodied their call to be unique in a prejudiced, elite way that presumed they were more loved by God than others. Too often God's people have more closely reflected images of empire, where fear, violence, competition, and exploitation are the primary liturgies.

The people of Israel experienced both sides of the empire imagination—from being enslaved to enslaving and dominating others. The Hebrew Scriptures bear witness to many who faithfully reflected God's image among the Israelites and beyond. They remain among the great cloud of witnesses for whom the church gives thanks. Despite the disobedience of many other leaders among the Jewish people, God's promise to use this unique people to spread salvation to all peoples of the earth was ultimately fulfilled in the coming of Jesus Christ.

It has been important, throughout Christian history, to worship Jesus without losing sight of his particularity— his history, his body. To nourish a robust understanding of what we think when we say "Jesus," we must begin with a theology of the incarnation, the story of Christmas, and the childhood of Jesus. Jesus was born into the blessed home of Joseph and Mary, nurtured, and eventually found his way to the Jordan River to be baptized by John. Then inextricably, empowered by the Spirit, Jesus was led into the wilderness to more fully discover who he was called to be and become. Encountering the particularity of Jesus invites the church to more fully consider who and what we are called to be as the martyr church of Christ's body.

The Salvific Nature of the Incarnation

Within Christianity there are always extremes and tendencies of unique emphases. Some parts of Christianity have celebrated Bethlehem as central to salvation. Salvation comes through the incarnation itself as God becomes truly human, healing the fallen nature of humanity through God's immersion into it. Other Christians have focused on Golgotha as the central story of salvation. Of course, while

Wesleyan Ecclesial Confession

Christ's coming is not an emergency operation or Plan B but part of God's plan to facilitate our ongoing growth and participation in God's love. This communion in God's love is possible through the incarnation, where God becomes fully human and makes possible our own full humanity, which is why salvation is aimed at helping persons become more fully human. Salvation is the healing of the disease of sin. In the coming of Christ, humanity can be transformed into what God fully intended for creation. Moreover, the affirmation that the incarnation was always part of God's plan also celebrates that the church as the body of Christ was not accidental. The gift of the church is part of God's plan for the healing of creation. The Son's incarnation in Jesus Christ is a further revelation of God and part of the new creation God is working in the world, which is the redemption of the cosmos.

some Christians emphasize one aspect over the other, it would be untrue to suggest that any parts of the church have dismissed the importance of the death and resurrection of Jesus, or the incarnation. However, it is problematic when Christians focus *more* on the need for Christ's death rather than celebrating the salvation that occurs from the beginning in *Immanuel*—God with us. Where sin caused disease and alienation between God and humanity, in and through the incarnated Christ that relationship is restored, and humanity is healed from sin to love.

Salvation is about a healing of sins—both what we have done and what has been done to us. Salvation also invites reconciliation—a union between God and humanity, through Jesus, by the power of the Spirit. Therefore, "the most basic reason for grappling with the historical question of Jesus is that we are made for God: for God's glory, to worship God and reflect his likeness."[1]

Mary and Joseph: Evangelists of the Martyr Church

Mary and Joseph serve as powerful evangelists—those who bear witness—to faithfulness in the martyr church. We are wise to examine the level of trust and obedience they both embody, for these are traits that offer lessons for the disposition of the church itself. The Gospels of Matthew and Luke celebrate the obedience of Mary and Joseph, inviting Christians to learn from and be empowered by their devotion and trust to God despite the risk to their lives. They opened themselves up to shame and empire violence for their willingness to participate in God's plan of redemption. Before Jesus could embrace *his* call to be the Messiah,

1. N. T. Wright, *The Challenge of Jesus: Rediscovering Who Jesus Was and Is* (Downers Grove, IL: IVP Books, 2015) Kindle Edition, 16.

Mary and Joseph had to embrace *their* call to raise the Son of God.

Mary: Favored Teenage Peasant

An angel's declaration of God's favor upon Mary brought confusion (see Luke 1:26–29). The angel invited her to be set free from fear and then talked about how God wanted her to participate in God's plan of redemption. While the confusion and anxiety certainly remained, Mary committed herself to the Lord's plans: "I am the Lord's servant. Let it be with me just as you have said" (v. 38).

This calling was blessed but would have brought difficulty from people with empire imaginations. Mary certainly would've experienced expressions of shame and disgrace by those who found her story unbelievable. The Law of Moses commanded death in the case of such obvious sin (see Numbers 5:11–31; Deuteronomy 22:20–21). Rabbinic practice in Mary's time did not encourage death, but as a presumed adulteress, "the penalty was still severe and humiliating."[2]

Beyond a fear of death, certainly anxiety over Joseph's response and their future life together must have weighed heavily upon her act of obedience. Mary's willingness to join in God's plan despite the threat to all she held dear parallels Jesus's prayer in Gethsemane as recorded in Luke 22:41–44. With a threat to be scorned, abused, humiliated and rejected by those she loved, she was willing and available.

Mary's devotion and trust must be seen as a foundation for the body of Christ and all who come after her as she responded to God's invitation to be used for the coming

---

2. M. Eugene Boring, "Matthew," in Leander E. Keck, ed., *The New Interpreter's Bible, A Commentary in Twelve Volumes: Volume VIII, New Testament Articles, Matthew, Mark* (Nashville: Abingdon Press, 1995), 134. See also Donald A. Hagner, "Matthew 1–13," *Word Biblical Commentary*, Vol. 33a (Dallas: Word Books, 1993), 18–19.

kingdom of God. Submission to God's will despite all the unknowns is a key aspect of life in the martyr church, and Mary embodied it fully. Though she did not seek death, she desired to be faithful to God even though it could have cost her life. Mary was asked to give birth to and become the mother of our Lord and Savior Jesus Christ at a time when giving birth was dangerous and the stigma of extra-marital pregnancy oppressive. Mary is an exemplar of the church as the body of the crucified and resurrected Christ.

Mary became the *theotokos* ("bearer of God"). As a young, female peasant in an occupied country, Mary demonstrated that the kingdom of God would come through those who are considered outcasts by empire standards. God, throughout history and still today, has often used people whom civic and even religious leaders overlook—people who have often been victims of the empire's obsession with power. In the martyr church we should be intentional about seeing that God is always present among those the empire relegates to insignificance.

Mary's obedience was an act of worship, embodied in the prophetic song known as the *Magnificat* (or "Mary's Song") in Luke 1. Mary's life celebrated that, though she was willing to join God's plan of redemption, she could not do it on her own. We can only live into hope and the calling of the martyr church when we rely on God's strength and empowerment. Mary's prayer celebrated what God was doing through her, the lowly and overlooked. In this way, her prayer was a prophetic statement about what God wants to do for all those the empire has deemed winners and losers.

> He shows mercy to everyone, from one generation to the next, who honors him as God. He has shown strength with his arm. He has scattered those with arrogant thoughts and proud inclinations. He has pulled the powerful down from their thrones and lifted up the lowly. He has filled the hungry with good things

Wesleyan Ecclesial Confession

Although God invited Mary to play
a crucial role in this salvation drama, it does seem
that Mary could have said no. We reject a notion
of God's power that is coercive and unable to
be resisted. We continue to see God's power
as invitational, something that empowers our
response without robbing us of making the
choice to participate. Affirming that Mary
could have said no highlights her faithful and
costly obedience in the martyr church.

and sent the rich away empty-handed. He has come to the aid of his servant Israel, remembering his mercy, just as he promised to our ancestors, to Abraham and to Abraham's descendants forever.

(Luke 1:50-55)

The *Magnificat* proclaimed good news to those who revered God properly, but it also warned the rich and the proud that the day of humble reckoning was coming. Perhaps the melody of this song sank into Jesus's bones, considering its primary themes were central to Jesus's ministry. In the first century—and sometimes in the twenty-first—those who were poor and diseased were thought to be under God's curse, while the healthy and rich were presumed to be blessed, holy, favored by God. The life and teachings of Jesus directly opposed this assumption. The message of the kingdom, which the church must continue to make creedal in imagination and practice, is that outward life circumstances are not always the best indicator of one's holiness barometer. Moreover, the gospel of the martyr church proclaims that God is not against—is not punishing—the poor and diseased. The rich also encounter grace with the reminder not to place their faith and trust in things that moth and rust can destroy and that thieves can steal (see Matthew 6:19–20).

The martyr church does not minister *to* the poor and oppressed; rather, the martyr church finds God centrally *as* the poor and *as* those marginalized by empire. The martyr church lives in and among those whom the empire considers the *least of these*. To be a member of the martyr church is to invite persons to become poor and marginalized in the eyes of the empire. The martyr church resists seats of power at the empire's table of control, violence, and exploitation.

Mary saw that this blessed calling in her lowly state was not about her alone but about what God wanted to say and do for all creation. God's calling and empowering of

Wesleyan Ecclesial Confession

The Scriptures are clear—God calls, equips, and empowers women for leadership in all levels of the church. In the martyr church all humans are uniquely gifted and empowered to lead. The martyr church must resist structures that exclude women from leadership.

Mary to participate in Jesus's life and ministry make clear God's desire for women to lead in the martyr church. Mary reminds us there is no inherent advantage to being male in the kingdom her child initiated. She was the first to welcome Christ, to extend and enable his mission, to offer hospitality to Jesus himself.

Joseph: Unexpected Father of God

Less is known about Joseph than we know about Mary. We can surmise he was probably much older than Mary. In order to pledge for marriage, a man would need to establish a career with enough resources to care for a wife and eventually children. A pledge of marriage in the first century was a public event, the beginning of a contract—much more than simply updating one's status to "engaged" on Facebook.[3] For Mary to have (or to be accused of having) sexual relations with any other man during the engagement (betrothal) period would not only cause Joseph great shame but would also be a serious breach of covenant.

The Gospel of Matthew offers the most detail for Joseph. Once he heard the news of Mary's pregnancy, Joseph legally had the right to expose her to public disgrace and more. Though he did not wish to shame her publicly, he did make a plan to divorce her quietly in order to honor the law (see Matthew 1:19). Joseph did not want to expose Mary as an adulteress, yet his devotion to his religion would not allow him to marry someone who was guilty of sin. "Joseph's plan expresses simultaneously his righteousness and his charitable kindness."[4]

While Scripture is not crystal clear about whether Joseph's intentions were known to Mary, it would be surprising if they were not. His decision to divorce her would be another layer of pain Mary would have endured in this

---

3. Hagner, "Matthew 1–13," 16.
4. Hagner, "Matthew 1–13," 18.

Wesleyan Ecclesial Confession

Regarding divine inspiration, if something is true and of God, it will be confirmed to more than one person. God is working in people as a collective, not simply in individuals with isolated truths. Resisting the allure of empire and living into the martyr church is difficult and, in some cases, not always easy to discern. Too often in my life I choose to put up blinders to the radical call of discipleship in the martyr church. I need others who are committed to the martyr church, first, to help provide the vision to see the road of discipleship and, second, the courage to embody it. Left on my own, I may lack the discipline and end up on the wide empire road that leads to destruction (see Matthew 7:14–15). Living into the martyr church requires communal listening to the Spirit.

drama. Yet, before it unfolded that way, an angel came to Joseph to encourage, command, invite him to take Mary as his wife. Joseph was let in on the secret that what was happening in her was from God and that she was telling the truth, which reveals another important characteristic of the body of Christ: mutual affirmation and confirmation (see more in the WEC). Joseph obeyed the angel and took Mary as his wife. While there was more at stake for Mary, Joseph's obedience is also worthy of admiration.

Flight to Egypt

The drama for Mary and Joseph did not end with her mysterious pregnancy. When the child was two, some magi from the East who were seeking the child brought gifts (Matthew 2:11). Another dream followed this unexpected blessing, in which an angel warned Joseph that Herod wanted to take the life of the infant king. Joseph and Mary escaped, finding refuge in Egypt. What became a place of slavery and despair for the Hebrews served as a sanctuary and means of grace for the holy family. Is it not just like God to redeem and transform prior places of pain and torture into safe havens of shelter?

Mary and Joseph refused to let their fear obstruct their willingness to participate in God's work of redemption through the incarnation of Jesus Christ. Their lives testified to the promise of the martyr church that faithfulness to God is better than securing our own safety through disobedience. By trusting God and refusing to be afraid of those who could use the sword to take their lives, they found life.

The path of the martyr church does not promise an easy life free of challenge but a life full of grace and truth.

Jesus: Life in the Martyr Church

Little is known of Jesus's life upon his family's return from Egypt to Nazareth before he began his ministry.

There were many infancy and apocryphal Gospels of Jesus written, but the church ultimately decided these were not needed or worthy of inclusion in the canon of Scripture. The Gospels are not biographies but testimonies and proclamations of whom they believe Christ to be. The words at the end of the Gospel of John are fitting: "Jesus did many other things as well. If all of them were recorded, I imagine the world itself wouldn't have enough room for the scrolls that would be written" (John 21:25).

Just as Mary and Joseph embodied key elements of the martyr church, the narratives of Christ's life are revelatory for what it means for his body to be the martyr church. Just like all of us, Jesus discovered God's call upon his life, and he faced the temptation periodically to choose a path of empire rather than martyrdom. Jesus was invited to yield his life to God by loving and serving those whom the empire threw on the trash heap. Jesus Christ refused the empire liturgy of fear and the temptation to find life by exploiting others; rather, he embraced the calling to find his life by giving it away in love and service to others. He loved and worshiped God by caring for and serving others.

In this journey through key moments of Christ's life, may we be further illuminated and empowered to follow God's invitation away from empire and into the martyr church.

Jesus Grows up Discovering God's Will

The Gospel of Luke provides unique details and stories about the childhood of Jesus. Luke celebrates Jesus's developing maturity. Christ's growth is more than marking his height each year on a doorframe. Jesus learns, matures, and discovers God's will for his life, just like every human does. After the encounter with Simeon and Anna in the temple, Luke celebrates, "The child grew up and became strong. He was filled with wisdom, and God's favor was on him" (2:40). After his twelve-year-old temple teaching, a story we'll explore in a moment, Luke notes, "Jesus matured in wisdom and years, and in favor with God and with people" (2:52). The point of emphasis here is that Jesus learns, grows, and matures—like all of us.

As truly human, Jesus is both the *model* and the *means* of salvation. Jesus's growth is a demonstration of God's power and strength. God's power and strength are made visible through humility and vulnerability. Christ, empowered by the Spirit, provides us encouragement, perseverance, and a *way* for us to follow. Just like us, he grew in wisdom and stature and worked to figure out God's call on his life.

The church must take keen interest in its charge to be the body of Christ, and to do this we must attend to what it means to *have* bodies. In Jesus's youth, having "the body of Christ" was for him not about powerful manipulation of the world but about humility, care, and earnest dedication to the will of the one he called Father.

Adolescent Jesus at the Temple

Luke 2 records that Jesus was with his family on their annual pilgrimage to Jerusalem for Passover. On the trip back home Mary and Joseph lost track of Jesus and eventually realized he must have been left behind in Jerusalem. Luke intentionally notes that Mary and Joseph found Jesus in the temple courts after *three* days. Jesus was lost to them for three days. This detail is not accidental but a clear foreshadowing of the time when Jesus will again be lost to his family and friends on the outskirts of Jerusalem for three days between his crucifixion and resurrection.

Jesus took the position of rabbi in the temple, teaching as one who had authority, even at a young age. This would not be his last visit to the temple, but it may have been the only visit he made when religious leaders were not against him.

Wesleyan Ecclesial Confession

As Christ grows and matures by the Spirit, so too can Christians grow and mature by that same Spirit in wisdom and favor with God and humanity.

John the Baptist

The Gospels of Mark and John have in common that neither one records a Christmas story, focusing instead on the ministry of John the Baptist, but Luke provides the most detail about the connection between John the Baptist and Jesus. John's birth recalled a familiar theme from the Hebrew Scriptures: God bringing life out of barrenness. Zechariah and Elizabeth were very old, and Elizabeth had never been able to conceive (see Luke 1:7).[5] This story of an old, barren couple experiencing new life certainly connects to Sarah and Abraham in Genesis 11. For the martyr church, these stories celebrate a God who invites persons who are considered barren by empire standards into promises that are impossible for people to achieve on their own. The martyr church is invited to allow God to work in places where all hope seems lost and to trust a God who is faithful. God's healing presence speaks hope into places of despair. This word of hope is not only for seeing impossible dreams come to pass but also for enduring pain and hardship.

John's life and message echoed the prophets who came before him, calling on the people of God to return to God. Anticipating that God's activity would include "judgment as well as redemption"[6], John proclaimed, "Change your hearts and lives! Here comes the kingdom of heaven!" (Matthew 3:2). John declared that God's reign of healing and restoration was coming *now*. John also challenged the Jewish religious and civic leaders who came to be baptized, pronouncing, "You children of snakes! Who warned you to escape from the angry judgment that is coming soon?

---

5. Modern science confirms that both men and woman can have issues that make it impossible to conceive, yet only women were blamed in ancient cultures for being unable to conceive. Infertility was a source of great pain and shame for women, a pattern that sadly persists today.

6. Hagner, "Matthew 1–13," 47.

Wesleyan Ecclesial Confession

God continually brings new life
out of barrenness and despair.

Produce fruit that shows you have changed your hearts and lives" (Matthew 3:7b–8).

What ultimately cost John his physical life was his judgment upon Herod, the puppet ruler of the Jews who was set in power by Rome. John charged Herod with adultery and breaking the law for taking his brother's wife, Herodias, in marriage. Herod arrested John and then had him beheaded at a party (see Mark 6:17–29; Luke 3:19–20). John preached a prophetic message that challenged the corrupt and brought a path to healing for those seeking it. John refused to soften the prophetic call to repentance and transformation even to those with empire power. John's commitment to preach against powers and principalities, even though it ultimately cost him his life, is a foundational characteristic of a member of the martyr church.

John's bold proclamation prepared the way for the Messiah—God's anointed, Jesus. (Matthew 3:3 declares that John fulfilled the role described in Isaiah 40:3.) Though he was literally tempted with a Messiah complex (see Luke 3:15), John the Baptist resisted. He clearly proclaimed, "I'm not the Christ" (John 1:20). John was faithful to his own calling and not the calling others tried to offer. John displayed his sincere humility by suggesting Jesus should be the one baptizing him when Jesus came to him and asked to be baptized (see Matthew 3:14–15). John's embodied humility and his assurance of his call from God—and, more specifically, what his call from God was *not*—are two more facets of the martyr church as distinguished from empire imagination.

Those with an empire imagination seek fame, power, and glory for themselves—often at the expense of others. This imagination not only exploits others but also sees others as competition and a threat. This devastating zero-sum game tricks participants into believing that their worth is somehow less when others receive praise because there is

Wesleyan Ecclesial Confession

Disciples in the martyr church never seek death but are willing to lay down their lives for the sake of the calling God places before them. Those with empire imagination who have power over others work to stay in power, and their gospel is to maintain the status quo. The martyr church of the kingdom of God works toward justice for all (righteousness) even if that means resisting the powers on earthly thrones—both civic and religious.

only so much glory and happiness to go around. The way of empire tells the lie that we must use fear to protect our fragile and insecure identities. Conversely, members of the martyr church find their identity solely in the life, death, and resurrection of Jesus Christ, finding joy in serving rather than in being served. The martyr church rejects the myth of scarcity to live in the bounty of God's grace, seeking to empower and praise others in a spirit of thanksgiving. To be great is to serve—without the need for empire recognition or honor (see Matthew 20:24–26).

Jesus's Baptism

The baptism of Christ offers three insights into the martyr church. John's ministry called for repentance, embodied in baptism, which would prepare persons for the work God was about to do. John recognized that Jesus was the "one whose way he was preparing."[7] As God's fulfillment, John the Baptist recognized that Jesus did not need to be baptized for cleansing and instead asked Jesus to baptize *him* (see Matthew 3:14).

Righteousness

The first insight affirms that Jesus refused John's request because Jesus's baptism was fitting to fulfill all righteousness (see Matthew 3:15). In the Gospel of Matthew righteousness is the goal of discipleship, which is the accomplishing of God's will.[8] God's will in the coming of Jesus was the kingdom of God irrupting on earth. Though Jesus was not baptized because he needed cleansing, his baptism was a central symbol of his willingness to submit to God's call upon his life as a Messiah who would live in solidarity with God's people, especially in their place of need. In baptism, this solidarity entered into the pain and

---

7. Hagner, "Matthew 1–13," 55.
8. Hagner, "Matthew 1–13," 56.

death of their sin in order that God may heal and redeem it. In this way Jesus continually laid down his life in love and service, ultimately culminating in his death.

The baptism of Jesus was the inauguration of his ministry and of the martyr church. Subsequently all Christians who are baptized in the name of the crucified God are initiated into the martyr church, fellowship in Christ's death and resurrection. Yet we are not left to navigate discipleship in the martyr church on our own.

Triune Revelation

Second, the baptism of Christ also becomes a revelation of the triune God—an event affirming the Father's love for Jesus and the beginning of Jesus's ministry. Though the baptismal accounts have minor variations, all three testify to the presence and voice of the triune God. As Jesus was baptized, the Spirit descended on him "like a dove" (Matthew 3:16; Mark 1:10; Luke 3:22), and the voice of the Father from heaven spoke: "You are my Son, whom I dearly love; in you I find happiness" (Mark 1:11; cf. Matthew 3:17; Luke 3:22).

Since baptism is initiation into the martyr church, the invitation to submit to God's call into God's kingdom is not a solo endeavor. When Christians are initiated into the martyr church at baptism, we are bound in covenant to the crucified triune God and to other members of the body of Christ. As members of the martyr church rise from the baptismal waters of death and chaos into our new cruciform life in God, we move out in the name of the crucified and resurrected Savior Christ, by the power of the Holy Spirit, with the blessing of the Father.

Mission

Third, these words of affirmation to Jesus from the Father send Christ and the martyr church out into the world to embody a ministry of hope, life, and hospitality through cruciform love. The refrain of divine Father claiming and/ or praising the son is an echo of Psalm 2:7 and Isaiah 42:1. Psalm 2 is a song of enthronement while Isaiah 42 is about the suffering servant. In his baptism, Jesus was enthroned as the suffering servant. This celebration of sonship was a summons to mission. At Christian baptism, all persons are named children of God and initiated into the martyr church, following the Messiah who loved so deeply that it cost him his life. [9] These words are both a blessing of welcome and a calling and commission to bear Christ's image in the world as the martyr church. Baptism into the martyr church is initiation into continuing the ministry of Christ to be present to those in pain and despair.

Temptation: From Wilderness to Gethsemane

In the afterglow of this holy baptismal moment, the Spirit, who fell on Jesus at his baptism, did not lead him to an earthly throne of power (empire imagination) but to the desert to be tempted (see Matthew 4:1; Mark 1:12; Luke 4:1).

Why include these temptations in the Gospels? What is the ecclesial importance of these temptations for the martyr church? Just as with the baptism, the temptations further confirm Jesus's allegiance to God in the cruciform calling. Is there some scandal and risk with Jesus's temptations? In the celebration of the humanity of Jesus, he was tempted and *could have sinned.* Jesus could have taken a path that was against the Father's will.

Christ was tempted to take stones and turn them into bread, violently objectifying creation to satisfy his own bodily needs. He was also tempted to test God by throwing

---

9. One of the most famous Trinitarian celebrations is found within the Great Commission and the charge to baptize persons in the name of the Father, Son, and Holy Spirit (see Matthew 28:19). This triune prayer for baptism was critical in the church's eventual theological affirmation of the deity of the Holy Spirit. See Basil the Great, *On the Holy Spirit* (Crestwood, New York: St. Vladimir's Press, 1980).

himself off the temple (often a punishment given for blas-
phemers), demanding God rescue and save him through
spectacle. Finally, the tempter offered Jesus a kingship of
empire where he could rule and have dominion over all creation as long as he (Christ) submitted to the god of empire.
These temptations tested Jesus's ability to discern whether
he would be a messiah of empire or of the martyr church.

Many Jews, including many of Jesus's own twelve
disciples, imagined a Messiah would come like a warrior—a
King David 2.0—and defeat all of their geopolitical enemies, specifically Rome, by use of the sword. This vision
was of an empire messiah in a kingdom of violence. Instead, the Messiah of the martyr church—the suffering-ser-
vant Messiah—would overwhelm and transform the world
through his *kenotic* love and humble service, viscerally entering into the pain and despair of those who suffered. The
empire conquers through the sword to silence those viewed
as a threat. The martyr church conquers through suffering
love and views none as enemies but all as made in the image of God and worthy of laying down one's life for.

Jesus found strength and wisdom to resist temptation
through Scripture and through the same Spirit who led him
into the wilderness. Even though his specific temptation
period in the wilderness came to an end after forty days,
Jesus was continually tempted, all the way to Gethsemane,
to be a Messiah of empire and not the martyr church. "After
finishing every temptation, the devil departed from him
until the next opportunity" (Luke 4:13). Yet, even as Jesus
was tempted and could have sinned, we affirm along with
the writer of Hebrews that "we don't have a high priest who
can't sympathize with our weaknesses but instead one who
was tempted in every way that we are, except without sin"
(Hebrews 4:15). The belief that Jesus was tempted continually but did not sin is a central ecclesiological affirmation.
Jesus *could have* walked down the path of empire, away from

kenotic and cruciform love. Yet, by the power of the Spirit, he continued submitting his life to the Father's will, beginning with the waters of his baptism into death and continuing all the way up to the chaos of death on the cross.

Christ's perseverance in faithfully leaning into the way of God becomes a source of hope and confidence for those who also desire to be part of the martyr church. Unlike the spirit of the Mandalorians in the *Star Wars* universe—who justify the killing of any who block their path—*Christ is the way of cruciform love.* The martyr church is invited and empowered by the Spirit to follow in hope and thanksgiving by laying down our lives, even for those who consider us to be enemies.

The garden of Gethsemane is another climax of temptations—when Jesus asked the Father to let the cup of suffering pass by him: "He said, 'Father, if it's your will, take this cup of suffering away from me. However, not my will but your will must be done'" (Luke 22:42). Even within this honest request, Jesus was willing to submit to the Father's will. Jesus refused to fight or to flee; instead, he followed the *kenotic* and cruciform love of God by allowing himself to be killed.

Jesus invites us to resist the seduction of empire with all its empty promises of comfort and peace through sword and coercion. Rather, we are invited to find life by taking up our cross and following Jesus into a life of compassion and presence to all, come what may—this is the martyr church.

FOUR

Disciples of the Martyr Church

Although few could have anticipated the intensity of ordinary simplicity that surrounded Jesus's birth, none could have imagined the horror of his death. Yet the Gospels are littered with Jesus's declarations to his disciples that he would be killed for his life and ministry:

> He said, "The Human One must suffer many things and be rejected—by the elders, chief priests, and the legal experts—and be killed and be raised on the third day." Jesus said to everyone, "All who want to come after me must say no to themselves, take up their cross daily, and follow me. All who want to save their lives will lose them. But all who lose their lives because of me will save them. What advantage do people have if they gain the whole world for themselves yet perish or lose their lives?
>
> (Luke 9:22–25)

Jesus knew it would cost him his life to faithfully live out his calling as Messiah—declaring, embodying, and living into the kingdom of God.[1]

Even though the disciples had a difficult time grasping this reality in the Gospels, Christian tradition bears witness that most of the disciples and hundreds of thousands of Christians were clear that living into this kingdom runs

---

1. Wright, *The Challenge of Jesus*, 3.

against the powers of oppression that are built on an empire liturgy of fear, intimidation, and violence. The church as the body of Christ unites with the crucified and resurrected Savior—hence, it is the martyr church.

The Blindness of Those Who See

Moving from fan of Jesus to follower (or disciple) in the martyr church is not easy. One of the gifts of the Gospels is journeying with Jesus's twelve disciples into the difficulty of navigating the call to discipleship. Mark 8 illuminates moments of both failure and faithfulness to discipleship in the martyr church.

Mark 8 falls within a section where lacking sense and ability was not simply physical but also spiritual. In the beginning of chapter 8 the disciples are invited to help feed the hungry crowd of four thousand. After an encounter with the Pharisees, Jesus warns the disciples about the "yeast of the Pharisees" (v. 15). The disciples kept worrying about the lack of physical bread they had with them and entirely missed the point (and perhaps also the real gift of feeding the four thousand). Jesus frustratedly asked, "Don't you have eyes? Why can't you see?" (v. 18a).

After the disciples' demonstration of spiritual blindness, in verse 22 Jesus and the disciples came to Bethsaida, where a man who was physically blind was brought to Jesus with the hope that Jesus might heal him. There are a couple of unique aspects of this healing story.

1) Jesus took the blind man's hand and led him outside the village. After spitting and laying his hands on the blind man, Jesus asked if he could see. (Why? Did Jesus not know? Whom was this question for?)

2) This healing happened in a couple of stages. The man's full vision was not restored until Jesus laid

his hands on him a second time. (Was Jesus losing his touch? Why the extra step?)

After Jesus's first touch, the blind man said, "I see people. They look like trees, only they are walking around" (v. 24). William Lane notes that this development likely indicates that the blind man once had sight and lost it since he knew what trees looked like.[2] Craig Keen suggests there is much more going on theologically than simply a multi-stage healing, offering an intriguing and creative allegorical interpretation. Keen notes that seeing people walking like trees is a connection to the overall theme of Mark 8 and the martyr imagination of entire Gospel.[3] To see people walking like trees symbolizes the many Christians who would be crucified for their faith on wooden crosses. The politics of the body of Christ is that of a martyr church. This interpretation is theologically creative and innovative, not commonly found among Markan scholars. However, developing the ability to see in stages connects powerfully to Peter in the story that immediately follows.

Right after the healing of the blind man on the way into the villages near Caesarea Philippi, Jesus asked the disciples, "Who do people say that I am?" (v. 27). Basically, Jesus was asking for the trending gossip about him. They variously answer Jesus with *John the Baptist*, *Elijah*, or *one of the prophets* (v. 28). Curiously, all these responses are of people who have already lived and died. In many ways, these answers lacked dynamic imagination, demonstrating that Jesus's identity was still hidden from the people.

Jesus then turned up the heat: "And what about you? Who do you say that I am?" (v. 29). In light of the disciples continually getting things wrong (just like us!), one might

---

2. William Lane, *The Gospel of Mark*, NICNT (Grand Rapids: Eerdmans, 1974), 285.

3. This interpretation was shared in personal conversation and reflection.

imagine a cautious response. One could also imagine that perhaps some of the answers they reported for the *people* could have included some of their own ideas.

The text does not give any clues as to how long there was silence, if there was any. In the same verse that Jesus asked the question, Peter responded, which could perhaps suggest an immediate, impulsive reaction: "You are the Christ" (v. 29). Immediately, just like the silencing of the demons in Mark 1:25 and his admonition to the healed blind man not to go into the village, Jesus commanded them not to tell anyone. It becomes more and more clear that one of Jesus's primary reasons for desiring this silence about his identity was that people simply did not know what it meant to be the Messiah.[4] Christ as Messiah was not David 2.0 who would conquer with the sword; rather, he conquered by laying down his life for both sinners and the sinned against.

This revelation was so difficult for the disciples to embrace. Mark 1:1 begins with the declaration that Jesus is the Christ—the Messiah and God's Son. Yet, after this bold proclamation at the beginning of the Gospel, there is no other confirmation of this confession until 8:29. This full confirmation by Jesus himself that he is the Messiah must have been a source of an even deeper joy and thrill for the disciples. The disciples knew that messiahs were powerful, wiping out enemies and receiving great glory, honor, and praise from the multitudes. The messiahs they knew won with violence. They certainly imagined that being part of his entourage would mean that some of the praise, honor, and power would splash onto them. Although they saw him cor-

---

4. It is noteworthy that in Isaiah 45:1, Cyrus is named as God's anointed, which is what "messiah" means. King Cyrus is credited with freeing the Jews from physical captivity and helping them rebuild the temple. As such, Cyrus was a king who did use the sword to defeat enemies who came in opposition.

rectly as the Messiah, they were still blind as to what Messiahship would mean—for Jesus and for themselves.

The entire Gospel of Mark shifts after Peter's proclamation in chapter 8 from celebrating Christ as Messiah through authority and power to revealing what it *means* for Christ to be the Messiah—then, by association, what it means for his Twelve and all who seek to be disciples. After Peter's declaration, Christ taught in Matthew, Mark, and Luke that he had to go to Jerusalem and suffer many things, including being killed and raised on the third day (Matthew 16:21; Mark 8:31; and Luke 9:22). This revelation certainly came as a shock to the disciples: "Jesus spoke of the necessity of his passion with a directness that scandalized the disciples (8:31–33)."[5] Since they had such high hopes of the empire glory they might receive by being close to Christ, they concluded that what Christ uttered must be false. The necessity of suffering and sacrifice is a key part of the revelation that the disciples failed to see.

Even though Peter confessed Christ to be the Messiah, he was blind to what that would mean for Christ and for those who follow him. And, although Jesus demanded silence about his messianic identity, he still spoke boldly and openly about the suffering he would endure, which was a deeper revelation of his Messiahship. As Lamar Williamson, Jr., put it, "Integrity in confessing the name of Jesus Christ is measured by consistency in following him on his way."[6]

In both Matthew and Mark, Peter heard Jesus's proclamation about suffering and firmly rebuked him (see Matthew 16:22; Mark 8:32). Peter's rebuke was certainly out of a deep love for Jesus, hoping to protect Jesus from harm. However, it was also a clear indication of Peter's own

---

5. Lane, *The Gospel of Mark*, 289.

6. Lamar Williamson, Jr., *Mark*, Interpretation Bible Commentary (Louisville: John Knox Press, 1983), 151.

Wesleyan Ecclesial Confession

One of the great temptations and dangers for Christians is that we tend to want to follow a more palatable God—one who will lead us to joy and prosperity. We must resist the temptation to mold Jesus into our own image of a God who is here to make our lives easier and more comfortable. True discipleship— articulated liturgically every Lenten season— is to follow Jesus to the shadow of the cross. Following Christ necessarily involves resisting the idols of making comfort and security our primary hope.

self-centered concern that if Jesus were killed, Peter and the disciples may face the same fate. What will be seen time and again is that—for Peter and for us—when fear takes hold and plants itself into our imagination, it often reaps a quick harvest of faithless disobedience.

Jesus matched Peter's rebuke with his own, even going so far as to call Peter Satan. Jesus did not call him Peter ("the rock"), or even Simon, son of Jonah. In this moment Peter was the presence of Satan, the adversary, who was tempting Jesus toward an empire path that was easier—a path where Christ would not need to lay down his life. Not only was this a temptation Jesus continually faced from the desert onward and had to overcome, but he also declared that all who would be disciples—citizens of the kingdom of God—must be just as willing to lay down their lives. Peter's declaration of Jesus as *Christ* did not mean Peter got to define what *Christ* meant.[7] The kingdom of God that Jesus inaugurated declares that those who are citizens of this kingdom can only find their lives when they are willing to lay down their lives. In this kingdom of God, the church of Jesus Christ is a martyr church.

Notice that Jesus did not banish Peter from his presence even when he called him Satan. Instead, Jesus said, "Get behind me" (Mark 8:33). In other words: *Be a disciple again. Follow me.* As we know, this was not Peter's first nor would it be his last misstep, but Jesus never gave up on Peter.

Let's consider again the physically blind man from earlier in the chapter who needed a couple of attempts from Jesus before he could fully see. With Peter in Mark 8, we see the very same phases of clear and blurry kingdom vision. Although Peter was able to testify and proclaim Jesus as the Christ, he also became Satan to Jesus in the very same event, demonstrating how blind he still was regarding his under-

---

7. Williamson, *Mark*, 153.

Wesleyan Ecclesial Confession

The church's true confession of beliefs
is not first about propositions that are stated but
lives that are lived. One's actions testify to one's
true beliefs. Our lives become our true confession
as to whether we believe Christ to be the Messiah.

standing of Messiah. The disciples throughout all the Gospels have a few moments of clarity, but they also experience their share of spiritual blindness.[8] This connection between Peter and the blind man offers wisdom regarding the ongoing growth of a Christian and the journey of discipleship.

Disciples of a Crucified Messiah

The disciples must have been stunned—first at Jesus's declaration that he would suffer, then his rebuke of Peter. Their hopes not only of Christ's glory but perhaps also of their empire glory had been scandalously shattered. The scandal was about to get even more intense.

Jesus followed up his rebuke by offering a teaching into what discipleship would look like for those who followed a Messiah who would suffer, be killed, and then raised to life: "All who want to come after me must say no to themselves, take up their cross, and follow me" (Mark 8:34). To be a disciple of the crucified Messiah is not about feeling sorry for Christ but is an invitation to follow him by also taking up one's own cross. Many of Jesus's teachings and ideas were pulled directly from Jewish Scripture and/or tradition, but this notion of taking up one's cross was new, original to Jesus with no precedent in Jewish literature.

We Christians who are living more than two thousand years later must resist the temptation to soften and sentimentalize Jesus's words, lest we miss the horror of his invitation. Notice in Mark 8:34 that the audience of Jesus's teaching is not simply the Twelve but the *crowd*—Jesus is addressing all who desire to be disciples. In a Wesleyan

---

8. Although the theme of blindness is central to Mark and the rest of the Gospels, we must note the ways such language can exacerbate ableist theology, connecting physical disability with spiritual sin in ways that are not appropriate. Great care and caution should be taken—and new interpretive metaphors considered—in order to not reinforce any sense that a physical disability such as blindness is in any way a spiritual deficit.

ecclesiology, taking up one's cross and following Jesus is the difference between being a *fan* or a *follower* of Christ.

To find life, disciples of the martyr church must be willing to offer their lives back to God in joy and thanksgiving. Anything less will miss the fullness of life in this kingdom of God and a failure of imagination of the full coming of the new creation. By illuminating what it means to be Messiah, Jesus silences false delusions of grandeur according to the kingdom of swords and empires and teaches what life in the martyr church means for him and for all who desire to be his disciples. Jesus "warns that [humans] who seek to secure [their] own existence by denial of his Lord bring about [their] own destruction."[9] The disciples who flee in the garden of Gethsemane fall to this temptation.

William Lane says, "The motive for denial of Jesus and his words is shame born out of an anxiety from one's life and a basic unwillingness to be made an object of contempt in the world. Ashamed of past association with the Lord, the decision to seek approval form the world rather than from him exposes the Lord himself to contempt."[10] In all times and places, this concern about contempt in the world is not simply about being called names; for Christians throughout the ages, it has meant physical death. One's life can only be saved as it is given for Christ. The martyr church is not about tossing away one's life. Being killed does not necessarily make one a Christian martyr. Only as one's life is offered *for the sake of Christ and the gospel* can that life be saved. Moreover, Christian martyrdom is not about being *killed* but about offering one's life back to God, come what may. When the Gospels were written and put in circulation, there was no longer any surprise at the reality

9. Lane, *The Gospel of Mark*, 308.
10. Lane, *The Gospel of Mark*, 310.

Wesleyan Ecclesial Confession

Jesus does not invite Christians simply to watch
him minister and suffer. To fully receive healing,
forgiveness, and embody true allegiance in Christ's
kingdom—to be part of Christ's crucified and
resurrected body—the cost of discipleship
in the martyr church is to take up
our cross and follow Christ.

that both Jesus and those who professed to be part of his body were part of the martyr church.

Certainly, there are places around the globe in the twenty-first century where taking up one's cross as a Christian could very well mean laying down one's life in physical death. One challenge is that in this same twenty-first century in other parts of the globe, some who desire to be counted as members of the crucified and risen body also have swords at their side. In these places, using a sword to defend one's life as a Christian is both accepted and considered admirable, representing a long-standing challenge for which I have not found an easy answer: Can people who seek to have their identity and primary allegiance to the crucified and resurrected body of Jesus Christ also endorse a kingdom whose primary politic is the sword, killing all who might oppose? Can I be both a member of the kingdom of the crucified and resurrected Christ and the kingdom of swords?

Desiring Kingdom Glory

Mark 10 offers another powerful narrative about failing to listen to and follow Jesus. The basic premise of this chapter is Jesus asking: *What do you want?* At the beginning of the chapter the rich young ruler was not willing to leave behind his wealth. Immediately after Jesus predicted for the third time that he would suffer and die in Jerusalem, James and John (in Matthew 20, their mother spoke for them) wanted seats of prestige and glory in Christ's kingdom but of course had no concept of what glory looks like in this kingdom.

As a current teacher and former youth pastor, I can certainly imagine the intensity of Jesus's exasperation over James and John's shortsighted request. They were seeking seats of power and glory that were precisely the *yeast of the Pharisees* that Jesus already warned them about in Mark 8! In the kingdom Jesus brings, all the glory is God's, and we par-

Wesleyan Ecclesial Confession

Those who read the Gospels may be tempted to think the Twelve were not very bright and lacked faith. Yet the Gospels also show that, even though the disciples continually failed, God did not give up on them, which reminds the church today that God does not give up on us. This is not an excuse for us to live unfaithfully on purpose but an assurance that God is always ready to help us live more faithfully. In this sense, even though Peter was called Satan and even though he betrayed Jesus the night he was arrested, God was always waiting with open arms. When we read in the Gospels about the disciples stumbling and bumbling, our proper response to this demonstration of grace is to give thanks that— just as God did not give up on them— God will not give up on us and can still use us for the kingdom. We are not disqualified!

ticipate through a life of joyful discipleship. Naïve James and John, responding to Jesus's question, "Can you drink the cup I drink or receive the baptism I receive?" (Mark 10:38) said, *Sure, no problem!* Curiously, this bold and confident statement was made by disciples who, up until this point, have been fearful and cowering at the thought of Jesus's suffering—let alone their own! Perhaps they still did not believe that Jesus's kingdom and their allegiance to it would be the way of cruciform love. Their confident response to *be able* to drink the cup lives within the same naïve ignorance of Peter's rebuke in Mark 8, believing that his ability to confess Christ as Messiah also meant he could exercise some control over what Messiah meant. Jesus did not call James and John Satan this time but offered a window into their future citizenship in the martyr church. Indeed, these two and most of the others would, in the end, physically suffer for their allegiance to this kingdom and its Messiah.

To show that James and John were not alone, once the other ten heard of their request they become angry—not, as one might hope, because of the foolishness of the request but because James and John got to Jesus first. Their grumbling demonstrates their persistent empire imagination. God's kingdom was still not being grasped and properly imagined by these disciples even as they headed toward Jerusalem (and toward the cross) with Jesus. God's political kingdom will be embodied by love and servanthood and laying down one's life at the hands of those who carry swords in the empires of this world.

After their grumbling, Jesus offered more revelation into the martyr church. "Whoever wants to be first among you will be the slave of all, for the Human One didn't come to be served but rather to serve and to give his life to liberate many people" (10:44–45). This is the politics of the martyr church. This is the shift from being a *fan* of Jesus to a *follower,* taking up our cross right behind Jesus.

Wesleyan Ecclesial Confession

For Christians today, the resurrection can seem mundane, a simple creedal confession. However, it was beyond the expectation and imagination for the first disciples that Jesus would be killed and then raised. The disciples knew full well that Jesus laying down his life was an invitation for them as well. How often does the invitation to Christianity today come with such horror and trepidation? Too often today we have focused simply on the good things God offers—forgiveness, hope, healing, and eternal life—while ignoring the true cost of discipleship. Too often we want to receive the benefits of Christ's ministry without taking up our own cross. True Christianity calls for a full offering of all of our lives to God, come what may. This is the hope and promise of sanctification. Perhaps we must raise the empire alarms more loudly in our evangelism and discipleship in the martyr church.

In Mark 10, the one who saw most clearly was not the rich young ruler or the Twelve but Bartimaeus. This son of Timothy is more often called the blind man in this story, for that is what he was to everyone but Jesus. When he heard that Jesus was coming he shouted, "Son of David, show me mercy!" (vv. 47, 48). The crowd told him to be quiet, but he persisted. Jesus told the crowd (who became his evangelists) to tell Bartimaeus to come to him. The next detail, though subtle, should not be missed. Bartimaeus threw off his cloak and went to Jesus even though he was still blind physically. The cloak was likely his only possession and means of warmth from the cold, and likely assisted in his livelihood by holding any money that persons offered to him. But he trusted Jesus. Jesus asked the question he has been asking the entire chapter: "What do you want me to do for you?" (v. 51). Bartimaeus said, "Teacher, I want to see" (v. 51). After Jesus healed him, "he began to follow Jesus on the way" (v. 52).

Where was Jesus headed? To Jerusalem to be killed. Bartimaeus is an important model for those who want to be part of the martyr church. The healing he received was not simply to make his life more comfortable and convenient; instead, it prompted him to follow Jesus right to the place of his death.

FIVE | The Passion of the Crucified God

In the Last Supper narrative, Jesus transformed a Passover meal into what the Christian church later named the Lord's Supper or the Eucharist. During the meal Jesus announced that one of them would betray him, alluding to Psalm 41:9, in which the speaker ate bread with a friend who betrayed him. Pheme Perkins notes that "since Jesus told his disciples that his death is imminent, betrayal makes the person responsible an agent in the crucifixion."[1] In many ways this responsibility became true for each of the Twelve and even for us today when we sin (see Hebrews 6:4–6). Each disciple protested that they were not the betrayer. Jesus then offered them the bread as his body and the wine as his blood. Surely this was a meal of intimacy with confusion swirling about. Perkins also notes that this liturgical practice of "handing the bread/body to the disciples may be an invitation to participate in Jesus's suffering (Mark 8:34)."[2] One of the key invitations of the Lord's Supper is that, as we receive the body and blood of Christ, we are invited to *become* Christ's body and blood. As Augustine prays, "become of what you partake."[3] Similarly, in baptism, Christians are initiated into the body of Christ by dying and rising with

---

1. Pheme Perkins, "Mark," *The New Interpreter's Bible, Volume VIII,* (Nashville: Abingdon Press, 1995), 703.

2. Perkins, "Mark," 704.

3. See specifically Augustine, *City of God,* chapters 6 and 10 and *Confessions,* books 7, 10, and 16.

Christ through the baptismal waters. This sacramental invitation is to take up our cross and follow Jesus, come what may. This is the political action of the martyr church.

Jesus and the disciples left the supper and traveled to the Mount of Olives. On the way, Jesus offered more devastating predictions that, in addition to the individual betrayal he already predicted, "You will all falter in your faithfulness to me" (Mark 14:27, referencing Zechariah 13:7).

Peter offered an arrogant rebuttal: "Even if everyone else stumbles, I won't" (Mark 14:29). Peter simultaneously declared himself resolute while also establishing his moral superiority over the other disciples.

Jesus looked at him with eyes full of pain and compassion and said, "I assure you that on this very night, before the rooster crows twice, you will deny me three times" (v. 30). Like most defensive and insecure persons, Peter doubled down, insisting he would let himself die before he would deny Jesus (see v. 31). Just as James and John in Mark 10 unknowingly confirmed their future of suffering, Peter also announced his. We can hear in Peter's assertion a continued failure to acknowledge the path of suffering love Jesus was on or understand what his allegiance to Jesus would cost him. Although Peter is said to have voiced this sentiment, verse 31 also notes all the disciples affirmed the same naïve, ignorant oath.

The Garden of Desertion

Jesus sojourned in song with the disciples to the garden. They did not march as a battalion of warriors but as a shepherd would guide sheep, by voice and lullaby. When they arrived at the garden, Jesus told the disciples to *sit* and *pray*. This is the last time in the Gospel of Mark that the group is called "the disciples" until 16:7, after the resurrection.[4] He gathered Peter, James, and John—the three who were last singled out on a different mountain for the Transfiguration (see Mark 9:2–8). He invited these three to be near him as his prayer opened into a vulnerability of groaning despair. Perkins suggests that this intimacy of being close to Jesus at prayer is another way they can "share in Christ's cup."[5]

The garden was another invitation to discipleship, to follow close to Jesus, to be present with him in his groaning prayer of his life being poured out. Yet, despite James and John's claims to be able to drink the cup of Christ's suffering and Peter's strong claim that he would not deny or betray even if all others did, they could not stay awake and commune with Christ in his dark night of the soul. They had not disciplined their lives to follow Christ in these intense moments of turmoil and grief. They fell asleep three times, even as Jesus asked Peter to keep watch and pray and not fall into temptation. These three lapses into slumber certainly foreshadowed the three betrayals that Jesus predicted at the Lord's Supper would come later that very night. By failing to keep watch the disciples failed to be present to Christ in his time of need and also failed to fully understand his suffering that leads to God's glory: "The sleeping disciples effectively abandon Jesus in his suffering."[6] The inability to stay awake was not simply about their about physical exhaustion; it also represented a spiritual inability to be present with Christ and willing to follow him and die for him.

Christ's prayers in the garden and on the cross were prayers of lament. Perkins notes that psalms of lament are righteous expressions of deep anguish (Mark 14:34);

---

4. Perkins, "Mark," 707.
5. Perkins, "Mark," 707.
6. Perkins, "Mark," 707.

acknowledgments of "God's power to save (14:36a); and acceptance of what comes from the hand of God (14:36b)."[7] Prayers of lament often included the accusation that one's friends had abandoned the lamenter.

Not only were the three disciples with Jesus in the garden not faithfully present with Christ, but their inability to pray also exacerbated their inability to respond well to the moments that soon came upon them. Even before the soldiers and the whipping, the disciples had already begun to abandon Jesus. Craig Hovey notes that, although Jesus offered this place of deep discipleship in Christ at the table, the disciples failed to drink deeply of the cup of Christ's suffering.[8]

Even though Jesus asked for the cup of suffering to pass from him, he was also resolved to be obedient to the end. This posture of Christ's prayer is not for Christ alone—all Christians are invited to present our requests and desires yet also be willing to embrace whatever God wills or allows. Frankly, this kind of obedience is hard! Jesus's own humility in this scene testifies that Christ had already begun to achieve the victory over sin and death in order to become both the *model* and *means* for all Christians who would follow. The Last Supper and Gethsemane became Christ's climactic willingness to submit to whatever comes.

Arrested from Discipleship

One can imagine the grogginess and, hence, chaos of the next moment. The disciples were waking from their sinful slumber with Jesus's words of disappointment. All of a sudden, the soldiers arrived, and chaos ensued. Another disciple—whose failure of Jesus was not to fall asleep in Jesus's time of need but instead to collude with the Jewish authorities—approached and betrayed Jesus with a kiss.

---

7. Perkins, "Mark," 707.

8. Craig Hovey, *To Share in the Body*, 81.

Wesleyan Ecclesial Confession

Laments are central for the martyr church. A lament is not pious whining about difficult circumstances. A lament is a cry to God in protest, pain, and despair. The church has too often silenced laments because it makes others (often those who enjoy the privileges of empire) uncomfortable. Laments are a worship of complaint calling upon God to move, act, be present. The martyr church must be especially attuned to the cries from those in pain and oppression as an act of solidarity in the hope that God will show up! In the end, laments also call the church to be present to the needs and hurts that often get drowned out by the droning on of trite praise from those whose lives are comfortable and easy in the empire.

Wesleyan Ecclesial Confession

Wesleyans teach that the church must resist the temptation to imagine we would have performed more faithfully than the disciples in the Gospels—even when it comes to Judas. While Judas's actions were reprehensible, could it be that his hopes were not that far from our own? Though Scripture does not provide much insight into Judas's motivations, it is possible that he was hoping to force Jesus to be the kind of Messiah that all the disciples were expecting out of Jesus. Perhaps Judas was tired of Jesus spending most of his time with the marginalized and not going after the "real" problem—the Roman occupation. Liberation from sin was fine and good, but the real liberation they needed—as many Jewish people saw it, not just Judas—was from the sword of Rome. It's possible that Judas's betrayal was his attempt to jolt Jesus into action, helping him become the warrior (King David 2.0) who would slay their geopolitical enemy. We should not be so quick to condemn Judas before we have considered the ways we've tried to force our Christianity to be what we want it to be. Why are we so passionate about who is elected to political office when we ourselves fail to care for our own starving neighbors? Most of us have committed the sin of trying to create Jesus in our image to fit our own vision for how we think the world should be. Judas and the disciple who struck off the ear of the servant of the high priest imagined an empire like Rome and a Messiah like Caesar even as they thought that's what they were trying to overthrow. Although we do not dismiss Judas's terrible betrayal, we ought to consider the ways we all have been Judas by trying to fit God into our own desires and timetables.

Matthew and Mark do not identify who brandished the sword that cut off an ear of the high priest's servant just as Jesus was about to be arrested, but John 18:10 reports that it was Simon Peter. If we trust John that it was Peter, then we find an interesting comparison: though Peter could not stay awake and practice the liturgy of prayer and companionship, he was more than ready to practice the liturgy of the sword. Jesus rebuked the action: "Put the sword back into its place. All those who use the sword will die by the sword" (Matthew 26:52). Craig Hovey prophetically notes that the way of the cross is the nonviolent revolution: "Users of violence have abandoned their crosses for more effective means of achieving results."[9] After Jesus healed the servant's ear, he was led away while all the other disciples scattered. Hovey notes again that those who fled were not choosing nonviolence; instead, they were living into the same logic of fighting—but realizing they would lose. "The disciples chose to secure their own fate on their own terms and cease following Jesus to the cross."[10] In many ways their weakness in falling asleep was connected to their weakness in abandoning Jesus rather than following—rather than being disciples. While Jesus was *arrested* by soldiers in the garden, the Twelve were *arrested* from their discipleship.

The Cry of the Rooster

In Mark, after Jesus's trial, the narrative flashes outside to the courtyard, where we find Peter. A servant girl was the first to claim he was with Jesus (14:66–67). Peter denied it, claiming to have no knowledge or understanding. The servant girl was not convinced, so she told those around her that Peter was connected to Jesus. Peter again denied it. In verse 70, the girl was far more convincing as the crowd near

---

9. Hovey, *To Share in the Body*, 47.
10. Hovey, *To Share in the Body*, 82.

him declared his association with Jesus. Peter's agitation appears to have boiled over in a rage: "I don't know this man you're talking about" (v. 71). Even though Peter knew he was lying, in another way, his own actions confirmed his complete lack of understanding of who Jesus was. His testimony that he did not know Jesus was spiritually true. He knew Jesus but really did *not* know Jesus.

This scene parallels Peter's harsh rebuke of Jesus in Mark 8, when Peter was incensed that Jesus would suffer and die. As we have already discussed, he was not concerned only for Jesus but also for himself. Mere hours before this denial, this same Peter boldly declared a willingness to die with Christ and, according to the Gospel of John, was willing to use a sword to protect Jesus. Yet when Peter was caught alone, his fear for his own life moved him to deny his discipleship. Then that rooster crowed. At that jarring noise testifying to the light of the new day, the rooster was also testifying to Peter's darkness as despair overwhelmed him: "And he broke down, sobbing" (14:72).

Killing Their Wounded

Before we look at the John 21 narrative of restoration, let's acknowledge the restoration that never happened. Growing up in the church, I was struck by how little compassion there was (and still is) for Judas. Perhaps for Christians, the act of Judas serving as an informant for a mere thirty pieces of silver is simply unforgivable. Maybe topping it all off with the kiss of greeting as a kiss of death in the garden simply leaves no space for sympathy for Judas. Yet were Judas's actions worse than Peter's? In the Gospels, the only thing we really see Judas do is this betrayal. Peter, on the other hand, while he did have some moments worth celebrating, also had several fantastic failures recorded.

One of the great dangers in life and in the church is playing the comparison game. As will be seen in the John

21 narrative, comparing ourselves to others often has devastating effects in all directions. Some who look at others they view as saints become easily discouraged, assuming they can never be as faithful or holy as that person. The opposite is also true. Some Christians look at others and say, "Well, at least I am not as sinful as that person." In both directions, comparisons are toxic. We should all lives the lives God has placed before us without comparing our setbacks, weaknesses, accomplishments, or strengths to others.

After the kiss, Jesus was arrested, and then later Judas experienced intense guilt and despair. According to the Gospels, the garden kiss was the last time Judas was recorded as being physically with Jesus or any of the disciples. Judas found no fellowship among the followers of Jesus but sought solace in returning the blood money he was given by the Jewish leaders—who also provided no comfort, no community, no penance. Judas was all alone in his despair, guilt, and shame, and it overwhelmed him to the point that he took his own life to stop the pain (see Matthew 27:3–5).

I have noticed a similar trend in the church and in civic politics in the United States. During my doctoral studies I lived in Chicago, where I observed how quickly politicians, even of the same political party, turned on another once they had dirt on a colleague. It was like sharks with blood in the water. In Chicago (and I am sure other places), the political machine kills their wounded. Sadly, the church often does the same. How often have local churches further alienated, marginalized, and ostracized those who are hurting? The painful examples are too numerous to count: a teenage girl pregnant and unmarried with nowhere to go; a wife who is blamed for her husband's affair; a young person experiencing questions about sexuality who only finds condemnation; a person experiencing depression and self-harm ideation who is told their faith is too weak; a family who must endure rumors and whispers about a wayward or rebellious child. Lord, have mercy.

Grace for All—Especially the Wounded

Two of my favorite parables form a powerful lesson for the church concerning Judas—the parable of the unmerciful servant in Matthew 18 and the parable of the workers in the field in Matthew 20.

In Matthew 18, Jesus encouraged his followers to lean into the power of forgiveness by telling of a servant who somehow owed the king a massive debt—imagine something that is completely unpayable for a blue-collar worker, millions of dollars. In that context, if a person could not pay a debt, both they and their family would go to jail until it was paid off—debtor's prison. In this case, the servant's inability to pay would've meant a life sentence. He begged and pleaded for mercy from the king, and the king—in an incredible act of mercy that kings weren't usually known for—pardoned the debt. That same day the servant who had just been set free found a fellow servant who owed him a day's wages—a pittance compared to the suffocating debt the first servant just had forgiven. The other servant also begged for mercy, but one who had just been released from a life sentence in jail threw his fellow servant into jail. News of this behavior got back to the king, who was furious.

The church must work with tenacity to not allow any more Judases to die alone in despair and desolation. Moreover, in light of Jesus's parable about the workers in the field in Matthew 20, Christians ought to take a hard and deep look at how those who were hired later in the day were treated by those who had been working all day. To fold the parable of the prodigal son in here as well, the workers (like the older brother of the prodigal) failed to see that to be at work in the master's field was the highest blessing and place of life. To be jealous over how the Father treats the

Wesleyan Ecclesial Confession

One who has embraced the forgiveness God offers will in turn be able to forgive and have compassion on others. The church is a place of grace. All of us have received healing and salvation we do not deserve. We embody the church of Christ when we show compassion and grace toward others.

prodigal or those hired at the end of the day is a failure to recognize the blessing of being in the presence of God. Too many of us think of heaven not as a gift but as something we earn. For the church as the body of Christ, the end goal of the kingdom of God is to be in and transformed by the presence of the triune God. The danger for Christians is when we think that we work in God's vineyard for the goal of that denarius. Rather, the goal and hope of working in the vineyard is to be with and in God's vineyard *with God*. There is no better place to be.

The church must not be in the business of killing our wounded. If that is how those who falter on the inside are treated, why in heaven's name would anyone on the outside want to be involved in such a community?

Resurrection Hope: Birth of the New Creation

The four Gospels make it clear that, just as none of the disciples imagined the horror of the crucifixion, they also had no expectation of the resurrection. The women did not head to the tomb in order to await his resurrection but to faithfully care for a dead body.

The glorious resurrection of Jesus Christ is the turning point in the entire history of all things. In God's resurrection of Jesus, the full inauguration of the kingdom of God came to earth! The new creation was birthed in Christ's resurrection. The resurrection did not reverse the crucifixion but brought new life to the one who laid down his life and defeated death.

This event provides not only healing and restoration from sin but also the church's commission as the martyr church. In the resurrection of Jesus, the church received its mission to participate in God's renewal of all things, and at Pentecost the Holy Spirit was poured out upon them to equip them to participate in God's continual coming of the new creation on earth.

The resurrection of Christ is *the* pivotal act of God that provides the hope, calling, and future for the church. It is the *hope* of the future that pierces the uncertain angst of the present. The resurrection is the hope of all that the martyr church is invited to become.

Deserters, Deniers, and Betrayers Restored

Although Peter's failures are unmatched, all the disciples scattered and fled the garden. Only the women and John were present at the foot of Golgotha. Only the women went to the tomb to care for the body on that first day of the week. In light of their obedient faithfulness, the women's reward was to be the first to encounter the risen Savior and to have been entrusted with the task of being the first evangelists of Jesus's resurrection to the men who had lost their discipleship. Yet God refused to let the disciples' failures have the last word. God invited them (and God invites us) back to discipleship. The Gospel of John offers a post-resurrection scene by the sea that celebrates the God who refuses to ever give up on us despite our failures.

John 21 describes one final encounter between the disciples and Jesus at the Sea of Tiberias, where Peter decided to go fishing. There may be a temptation to over-read or under-read this text. Was Peter looking for a diversion, or was his return to fishing a reversion from Peter the disciple to Simon the fisherman? Others joined Peter, including his original fishing partners, James and John, and a few other disciples. Even though Peter denied Jesus, it appears he still held a level of leadership among the disciples. One possibility is that the other disciples were not aware of his denials since none were recorded as being with Peter outside the temple courts. The more likely scenario is that, since all the disciples scattered from Jesus when he was arrested, they all embodied a layer of guilt and shame. Perhaps in their minds Peter's denials were no worse than what any of the rest of them did at the intense climax of Jesus's passion.

As the story unfolds, it seems the professional fisherman had lost their touch. In the early morning, someone (the reader is told it was Jesus yet his identity was as yet unknown to the disciples) called out from the shore, asking how many fish they had caught. Like someone having to admit their golf score was in the triple digits, the disciples confessed they had caught nothing. This stranger on the shore invited them to cast their nets on the other side of the boat. Without any apparent reservation they followed the stranger's advice.

This scene certainly echoes and mirrors the story told in Luke 5, where Jesus went out on Peter's boat to fish. In the Gospel of Luke, Simon, James, and John were already back on shore and cleaning their nets after catching nothing when Jesus asked to go fishing. In the Gospel of John, they were still in the water. In both Gospels, after they followed Jesus's instruction, there emerged a catch of fish beyond what any could ask or imagine. In Luke, the surplus brought Simon to his knees in confession of sin. Without denying Simon's sinfulness and unworthiness Jesus said to him, "Don't be afraid. From now on, you will be fishing for people" (5:10). The invitation to *follow me* is implicit in Luke. The text simply notes that the disciples brought their boats to shore and left everything and followed Jesus. In one of the beautiful tapestries of the Gospels, this story told in the Gospel of John occurred at the very end of Jesus's earthly ministry—and, perhaps, what Peter thought was also the end of his discipleship after his fervent denial of Jesus.

Rather than the bounty of fish causing him to confess his sin as in Luke, in John 21 it caused "the disciple whom Jesus loved" to declare, "It's the Lord!" (v. 7). Peter's response was a combination of joy and compulsive action. He simply tied a coat around his waist and jumped in the water, leaving everything else behind. This response is perfectly recast in the motion picture *Forrest Gump*, when Forrest sees his beloved Lieutenant Dan on the dock waiting for him. Forrest abandons his shrimp boat as it is still coming in from the sea. He jumps off the moving boat, leaving it without any crew, diving into the water in order to get to Lieutenant Dan as fast as he can. After Forrest emerges from the water and climbs up the dock and greets Lieutenant Dan, Forrest offers a face of joy that must have matched Peter's joy and excitement to see Jesus. Jesus invited them all to bring some of the fish they caught to the fire and join him for a breakfast he had already prepared.

The Thread of Three

John 21:14 notes that this was the *third* time Jesus appeared to the disciples after the resurrection. This number three is like a scarlet thread woven all through the Gospels. Jesus was missing from his parents for three days in the temple at Jerusalem when he was twelve (Luke 2:41–52). The Adversary offered Jesus three temptations in the wilderness (Matthew 4:1–11). Peter denied Jesus three times before his death (Mark 14:66–72). Jesus was dead for three days before his resurrection, which Jesus himself connected to Jonah being in the belly of a fish for three days (Matthew 12:38–42).

After breakfast in John 21, Jesus engaged Simon Peter directly. "Simon son of John, do you love me more than these?" (v. 15). What does the phrase *more than these* refer to? There is not consensus among scholars about whether *these* refers to Peter's love for Jesus (did Peter love Jesus more than Peter loved the other disciples?) or the disciples' love for Jesus (did Peter love Jesus more the other disciples loved Jesus?). Recall that Peter responded on the night of Jesus's arrest that he would not fall away *even if all the other*

Wesleyan Ecclesial Confession

Without Jesus, the disciples would not have caught any fish. Yet, when they trusted and relied on Christ's direction, God led them to a bounty beyond compare. Even though Jesus had already prepared breakfast and did not need the fish that had been caught, he still invited them to contribute. Jesus desired their participation in the meal of reconciliation. God desires to partner in the further healing and redemption of creation. Though God and humans do not partner with equal power, from Adam and Eve through Abraham, Isaac, Jacob, Moses, Rahab, Joshua, Gideon, Ruth, Isaiah, and more, all the way to these disciples, God continually invites humans to participate in the redemptive work God is doing in the world. Part of humanity's ongoing healing and salvation is connected to our joyful work participating in God's missional work of the redemption of all things. Within the strong affirmation that God does not force or coerce creation into healing, the Spirit-empowered response of humans to participate in God's work is part of the gift and calling of the church.

disciples did. The implication was that Peter thought his love for Christ was stronger and deeper than all the other disciples. So Jesus may have been asking Peter, after his three denials, if he still thought he loved Jesus more than everyone else.

These may also refer to Peter's fishing equipment. More than merely gear, it represented his life and identity before Jesus. Whatever Jesus may have been referring to, "Simon replied, 'Yes, Lord, you know I love you.' Jesus said to him, 'Feed my lambs'" (v. 15). Jesus addressed him not as Peter but as Simon—his old name. In John 1:42, Jesus changed Simon's name to Cephas/Peter—"the rock"—yet here Jesus called him Simon. These are the first recorded words of Peter back to Jesus since Jesus told Peter he would betray him on the night of his arrest. Simon was his life and his identity as a fisherman before he was Peter the disciple.

Peter's bold response, even after his three denials, is presumptuous. Words come easy, but Peter's actions demonstrated a deep lack of love for Christ, so Jesus asked him a second time, and he responded the same. Jesus told him, "Take care of my sheep" (21:16), then asked a *third* time. The Gospel notes that Peter was *sad* at Jesus's continued questioning. No doubt, he recognized that the three questions matched the number of his denials, and the sadness, shame, and guilt under the surface began to bubble up.

In his third response, Peter did not draw upon his own words but appealed to Jesus's knowledge that could testify to Peter's love for him. Jesus again commanded Peter to feed his sheep but then elaborated on what it would cost to love Christ and care for God's flock: "'I assure you that when you were younger you tied your own belt and walked around wherever you wanted. When you grow old, you will stretch out your hands and another will tie your belt and lead you where you don't want to go.' He said this to show the kind of death by which Peter would glorify God. After saying this, Jesus said to Peter, 'Follow me'" (vv. 18–19).

Jesus never denied Peter's claim to still love Christ. Yet he was still trying to teach Peter what it means to truly love Christ. Peter, who was afraid of a servant girl finding out his identity in the courtyard, needed to understand that to love Jesus and to care for his sheep meant there would come a time when following Jesus would cause him pain. In case there was any doubt, in verse 19 John clarifies for the reader that Jesus's words to Peter were connected specifically to how Peter would glorify God through death. Then Jesus looked at Peter.

Imagine you are Peter. Jesus looks at you. What are Jesus's eyes like in your mind? In my imagination, Jesus's eyes hold so many emotions. First, his eyes show compassion, mercy, forgiveness toward Peter for his denial of Jesus and renouncing of his discipleship; for his failure to stay awake in the garden; for using the sword in the garden; for his fear of empire in the questions of a lowly servant girl. Second, I imagine Jesus's eyes are also filled with sadness, recognizing what it will mean for Peter to truly be a disciple, to truly love Jesus, to deeply care for his sheep. Third, I also see Jesus's eyes as filled with hope that Peter—despite the failures of the past and the hardships of the future—will become a disciple again.

This is not a God of retribution. This is not a God of forceful control. This is not a God who lets our failure be the last word. This is the God of loving invitation. Even though being a disciple is not the road of least resistance, it is the road to life (Matthew 7:13–14). Of course, Jesus's invitation was not just for Peter but for all who lost their discipleship in the trial of Jesus's passion—and of course it is for us today!

At this point in John's narrative, I am cheering for Peter to respond to Jesus's invitation to follow with a slow and thoughtful, "Yes, Lord." I wish verses 20–24 did not exist. The Gospel could end prophetically and powerfully with this invitation Christ gives to all in verse 19: "Follow me." But Peter—God bless Peter—one more time he had to show he still had a long journey ahead of him (just like all of us). Peter tried to play the comparison game once again, asking, "Lord, what about him?" While the call for all Christians is a willingness to follow Christ come what may, each Christian's journey living out a love for Christ will not be the same. The key is to be willing—out of deep love and gratitude to Christ—to pick up our cross and follow him. Our eyes should be on Christ, not distracted by the unique journey each sister or brother will take as they carry their own cross. To love Christ—to take care of and feed his sheep, to follow Christ—is to join in his body that was crucified and resurrected. This is the martyr church of Christ.

Christ by the Spirit looks at each of us and asks, *Do you love me? Then feed my sheep. Do you love me? Are you willing to yield your life to God as an offering of thanksgiving? Do you love me? Will you follow me?* This invitation still stands for us each day. Even if we have failed in the past and feel we are unworthy of the calling, God invites us toward repentance and again to pick up our cross and follow. This is the martyr church—the body of the crucified and risen Christ.

The Spirit as the Power of the Martyr Church

The Gospels are the celebration, proclamation, and revelation of Jesus as the Christ, the Messiah of God. The Son was sent with the Spirit by the Father for the deep healing and redemption of all things as the inauguration and irruption of the kingdom of God. Sometimes we miss a key emphasis of the Gospels, celebrated most specifically in the Gospel of Luke, regarding the Spirit's empowerment of Jesus throughout his ministry. As Wesleyans we would not say the Spirit was *absent* before Jesus's baptism, but at the baptismal scene, the Spirit fell upon Jesus in a unique and powerful way. The Holy Spirit then led Jesus into the wilderness to be tempted. Later, in the reading of Isaiah in his hometown synagogue, Jesus testified that the Spirit of the Lord was upon him. From birth through baptism, all the way to the cross and into the resurrection, the Spirit's empowerment of Jesus remained steadfast.

Another gift of the Gospels and all of Scripture is the testimony of people on their journey with God. We see the faithfulness of some empowered by the Spirit, specifically Mary (Luke 1:35); Elizabeth (vv. 41–45); and Zechariah (vv. 67–80) However, in addition to these Spirit-empowered successes, there are also accounts of some fantastic failures, not only by those who consistently opposed Jesus (like the Jewish religious leaders) but also by those closest to him, like the Twelve. The gift of these failures is that for most of them, as my colleague T. Scott Daniels keeps encouraging me, *our failures do not have to be the last word.*

Not only do the Gospels powerfully reveal Jesus the Christ, but they also demonstrate the significant power and effect of Pentecost in unleashing the Spirit upon the church. This entire conversation about the church as the body of the crucified and resurrected Christ is done by the power of the Holy Spirit. Unfortunately, although Easter is rightfully celebrated as a high point in the church year, Pentecost often gets lost or forgotten in the Western church.

The problem, of course, is marketing and consumerism. Taking some hints from Christmas and Easter, all Pentecost needs is a simple marketing strategy. If we created a mythical creature to bring children chocolate and presents, Pentecost could take off. The creature could be a dove that is always on fire without being consumed, and it drops candy and gifts on the heads of all those ready to receive. Perhaps with the power of consumerism behind it, Pentecost can finally receive the attention it deserves!

Pentecost is the birth of the church, the unleashing of the Spirit. The Spirit is the power and presence of God that enables, inspires, equips, interprets, and illuminates *all* that the church is and does. The importance of the Spirit cannot be overstated. Too many of us neglect the Spirit even as we rightfully worship God the Father and God the Son incarnate in Jesus. It's possible that the nature of the Spirit makes us nervous sometimes. After all, the Spirit cannot be tamed or controlled. The Spirit invites the church into courageous action. While God is a God who orders chaos, remember that the event of Pentecost allowed persons to understand in their own language. Diversity was blessed, not dismissed. Unity in the Spirt is not stringent uniformity.

Christ's Promise of the Spirit

In John 14, Jesus talked about going ahead of the disciples to prepare a place for them (v. 2). Thomas of course asked about the GPS directions. *Christ, what is the address so we can track you down?* Jesus then celebrated the unity between himself and the Father. But then he made a truly remarkable claim that many Christians probably do not really believe: "I assure you that whoever believes in me will do the works that I do" (v. 12). *Really?*

For the disciples who truly wanted to believe, continuing the works that Christ did may have seemed an impossible task. They had a hard enough time simply understanding what he was teaching. As the Gospels push closer to Jesus's passion it feels like the disciples became less and less competent. Are we any better in the church today? Sadly, it feels like today we are known more for our infighting and judgment rather than for continuing the works of Christ. This statement from Jesus feels like a hopeful exaggeration more than a reality. But then Jesus said something utterly ridiculous: "They will do even greater works than these because I am going to the Father" (v. 12). Clearly Jesus had lost it by this point. No way! Walking on water, healing infirmities, challenging rulers and authorities with love? Simply *matching* Christ's works feels like a reach, but doing *greater* works is impossible!

The What

Before going any further, let's address another conversation we often hear both inside and outside the church. If the church is the body of Christ, why are there no more miracles like Jesus performed? Why can't Christians make the blind see, the lame walk, and cure diseases on the spot?

Often the idea of *miracle* is equated with a suspension of natural law. However, Jesus's messiahship was not about magic tricks; it was about helping guide the disciples into places of faith they never knew they could go—and also showing them how far they had yet to go. Moreover, Jesus's healing of physical maladies was not simply to make lives easier but to affirm the love of God in people's lives and to show that God was Lord of all disease.

All of this does not mean God is not still performing miracles today. Whether by medicine or by prayer, God continues to offer healing to physical bodies.

Prayers for Healing

The church has often squelched the tendency to pray for physical healing because it is messy. One of the great privileges of a pastor is praying *with* and *for* people. One Sunday morning I prayed with one of our saints at the altar. She was having some internal bleeding, and the doctors were concerned. I anointed her and prayed that God would heal her. When I saw her the next week, she told me all the internal bleeding had stopped, and the doctors were baffled. She was healed! To be honest, I was a bit stunned—not because I did not believe God could do it but because, in my experience, God does not often work in that way. I have prayed for many others with physical needs who did not see such immediate release.

Even though prayers for physical healing are messy, we should keep praying them. We are also reminded that success in prayer does not mean we got God to do *what* we wanted *when* we wanted it. Rather, prayer's full hope is in how persons are bound together in God and transformed as we journey through life. Our prayers are not magical incantations. God sometimes does heal through prayer or medicine, and other times God heals by allowing someone's journey in this life to end. But the church should continue to pray with boldness (James 5:14–16).

When John the Baptist questioned whether Jesus was the Messiah, "Jesus responded, 'Go, report to John what you hear and see. *Those who were blind are able to see.* Those who were crippled are walking. People with skin diseases are cleansed. Those *who were deaf now hear. Those who were dead are raised up. The poor have good news proclaimed to them'*"

(Matthew 11:4–5). The Messiah was about liberation. The notion of the dead being raised and the poor hearing the good news leans into a key part of this present and future coming kingdom.

Remember that all the persons Jesus physically healed—the blind, the lame, and mute—eventually died. Even Jairus's daughter and Lazarus, whom Jesus raised from the dead, still died again at some point (by the way, this is why we should not say Lazarus was resurrected but that he was resuscitated). The real miracle that Jesus began in the inauguration of the kingdom was sinners finding forgiveness, healing, and transformation.

The gospel is that victims who have been sinned against find Christ present in their suffering and despair, inviting them to hope beyond their despair. Kingdom miracles are not attempts to fabricate party tricks by breaking natural laws but participation in people's liberation. Addicts finding peace and recovery. Those who have been abused learning to love themselves and lean into God's love. Enemies reconciling. Eradicating injustice and oppression. Physical healing in Jesus's context also had an added layer due to a widespread error in ancient belief that physical maladies were deserved: when Jesus physically healed someone, it was a divine proclamation that God was not against them, was not punishing them, had not forgotten them—but loved them.

Clearly the emphasis that the church will do *greater works* is not on the claim that the church can do more based on its own power or ability. Rather, these *greater works* are all about the kingdom that Jesus began that is still growing and expanding long after his death, resurrection, and ascension.

The How

But how? In the very same passage in John 14, Jesus announced how this can be by sharing that, after Jesus left,

the Father would send the Companion/Helper/Advocate—
who would be with us forever (v. 16)—the Spirit of Truth,
who was not only present but also already lived in the
disciples (v. 17). This Companion would continue teaching
and reminding them of everything Christ taught (v. 26).
This reminding is not simply about mental recollection;
the church would later affirm that the Spirit empowers us
to live out the crucified and resurrected life of Jesus. The
disciples were empowered to continue the ministry of the
incarnation and participate in God's further bringing of the
new kingdom as the Spirit continued to be unleashed. Since
we have considered Peter's epic failures in the Gospels, let
us also consider the ways Peter was transformed by the
Spirit in Acts.

The Spirit's Empowerment of Peter

The presence and power of the Spirit were boldly seen
in Peter in the sermon he preached on the day of Pentecost
in Acts 2 and in those who were physically healed. Even
though Jesus gave the disciples authority over unclean spirits and disease and sickness (see Matthew 10:1; Luke 9:1),
there are no healing miracles by the disciples recorded in
the Gospels. The only story recorded is about the time they
failed (Matthew 17:14–20; Mark 9:14–29). Yet, after Pentecost, Jesus's promise was realized in Acts 3.

Peter and John were going to the temple to pray and
came across a man who had been disabled since birth. The
man asked for what he thought he needed most—money,
probably for bread and other life necessities. Peter and John
did not have any since those were all shared communally
(see Acts 2:45). Yet Peter replied boldly, "Silver or gold I do
not have, but what I do have I give you. In the name of Jesus Christ of Nazareth, walk" (3:6, NIV). When the man got
up, the first thing he did in the wake of God offering him a
gift beyond his imagination was walk with Peter and John
into the temple to praise God. This story follows a very sim-

Wesleyan Ecclesial Confession
Everything is interconnected.
God does not offer physical healing simply
to make our lives easier but to affirm that
God is Lord of sickness and to invite persons
into receiving physical healing by offering
all of their lives back to God in full
worship and discipleship.

ilar theme to the healing of blind Bartimaeus in Mark 10, who followed after Jesus along the way once he was healed. Both stories underscore the emphasis that physical healing in the New Testament invited individuals into deeper levels of discipleship.

In our discussion of Peter, it would be dishonest to suggest that the Spirit's coming at Pentecost meant that nobody got nervous about their situation or their calling ever again, but one of the gifts that Pentecost offers is the invitation to discard fear.

Distinguishing fear from being scared is important. While these distinctions are only mine, it may help understand what I'm getting at. I think of being scared as being startled, something happens quickly, like when someone jumps out at you in the dark and scares you momentarily, or when my wife screams because a spider surprised her. When I talk about fear, however, I am thinking about an overall sense of doom and despair that can hold persons captive and oppress them by trapping them in cycles of withdrawal, disobedience, and sometimes violence.

Using this distinction, one can imagine that the disciples would've been startled, or scared, when Jesus appeared to them suddenly in the upper room after his death. This emotion was much different from Peter's denial that he even *knew* Jesus outside the temple. Peter's repeated denial of Jesus was an action of *fear*. One of the striking transformations in Peter following Pentecost was his willingness to proclaim the gospel even when it may cause him harm.

After the healing of the man in Acts 3, chaos erupted when the man walked into the temple with Peter and John. He likely had been a fixture outside the temple for some time, and now that he was inside, standing and walking on his own, the news was going viral. Peter, never one to waste a moment, used the opportunity to preach again about Jesus, and he did not shy away from the uncomfortable truth that among his listeners were some who were responsible for Jesus's death. He boldly proclaimed that they had willingly "killed the author of life" (v. 15). Peter's goal was not to condemn but to invite them to repent (v. 19).

Nonetheless, the religious leaders were displeased and seized Peter and John and put them in jail (4:3). The next day they were brought before the Sanhedrin to be questioned. When asked by what power they preached, Peter wasted no time in offering a response that was "inspired by the Holy Spirit" (v. 8), and he again preached about Jesus to this powerful body—the same people Peter said the day before had "acted in ignorance" (3:17).[1]

The members of the Sanhedrin were *surprised* by Peter and John's confidence: "After all, they understood that these apostles were uneducated and inexperienced. They also recognized that they had been followers of Jesus" (4:13). Even though Peter and John had been followers all along, the equation of time plus influence plus the fresh infusion of the power of the Spirit yielded a new and prophetic boldness. Filled with the Spirit, Peter declared that Jesus Christ, "whom you crucified but whom God raised from the dead" was "the cornerstone" (vv. 10, 11). May the church today live out Peter's confession in hopeful joy. "Throughout the whole world, no other name has been given among humans through which we must be saved" (v. 12).

The religious leaders had no clue how to handle these upstarts, yet the man who had been disabled was right there as a living testimony to the very gospel of Christ they were proclaiming. They warned Peter and John not to speak in Jesus's name any longer. But Peter and John—one of whom fled on the night of Jesus's arrest and the other who

---

1. Robert W. Wall, J. Paul Sampley, and N. T. Wright, "Acts," in *The New Interpreter's Bible, Volume X: Acts, Introduction to Epistolary Literature, Romans, 1 Corinthians* (Nashville: Abingdon Press, 2002), 89.

feared a servant girl in the courtyard—spoke with power and conviction: "It's up to you to determine whether it's right before God to obey you rather than God. As for us, we can't stop speaking about what we have seen and heard" (vv. 19-20). In this scene, and many others, Peter and John resisted fear of what the Sanhedrin might do to them. By the Spirit, they refused the temptation to fear and trusted in God to live as faithful witnesses of Christ. They knew that obeying God was the only way to real life. In this moment they were picking up their crosses and following Jesus. They had gained their lives because they were willing to give them away. Peter and John's actions were a perfect example of the martyr church refusing the empire's liturgy of fear.

The coming of the Spirit in Acts did not mean that all difficulty and challenge ceased; however, a new day had dawned. These men who were once afraid were now seeing God's healing Spirit of Christ flow through them both in physical healing and prophetic preaching to all who had ears to hear. No matter what may come, even under the threat of losing their own lives, the disciples could not and would not stop speaking about this Christ who had transformed their lives and who desired the healing of the nations.

As absurd as the disciples believed Jesus to be in John 14, what about Christians in the twenty-first century today? Do we believe that Christ's promise about the gift of the Spirit is still true? Are we willing to proclaim the good news of Christ, even if that means potential hardship in the face of powers and principalities? I am afraid, in the paraphrased words of Stanley Hauerwas, that Christians have given the world too little to be afraid of, to resist, to be bothered by. We have too often been the grease in the wheels of empire.

Yet today is upon us. How do we live empowered by the Spirit in prophetic hope and courage to love and proclaim the power of the gospel of Christ as the church more fully becomes the body of the crucified and resurrected Savior?

Life in the Body

With a strong foundation in the life of Jesus and lessons from the disciples, the conversation now turns to the martyr church today, concerning how the triune God is still at work in the world drawing and wooing the church to more fully be the body of the crucified and resurrected Christ.

This section explores the God who calls women and men into lay and clergy leadership in the church. It also explores healthy and toxic leadership and how to address conflict in the church. Section 2 will close with a serious reflection on the ways the church has been an agent of harm and pain in the lives of hurting people.

SEVEN

Come and Follow Me

In the first century, while there was not a regulated practice, it was common for potential disciples to seek out a rabbi to be trained in that particular rabbi's school of thought. Rabbis often chose the best and brightest, those who showed the most promise to carry the school of teaching forward for future generations. Those who didn't excel often opted out (or were opted out) as a sign that other professions would be a better fit.

Jesus did things differently. Instead of waiting for disciples to choose him, he reached out and selected his own; not only that, but those he chose were not the best and brightest. The disciples he chose did not have the regular or even recommended pedigree. We do not know a great deal about most of the disciples. We know that Andrew, Peter, James, and John were fishermen and that Christ called them to start fishing for people (Matthew 4:18–22; Luke 5:1–11).

The Gospels also record the calling of Levi/Matthew, a Jewish man who was despised by his own people because he was a tax collector (Luke 5:27–32). The fishermen were common people, not extraordinary in any particular way, but Levi was worse than common: he was seen as a traitor, having sold himself to Rome in a profession that exploited his fellow Jews. Yet Jesus invited him as well.

Jesus invited people to find unity when enmity would have been their first response. Matthew lists Judas as the one "who betrayed Jesus" (10:4). His inclusion in the list of

Wesleyan Ecclesial Confession

Scriptural witness shows that God does not call the qualified but qualifies the called. Throughout Scripture, God calls people whom everyone else would and did overlook. Our past failures or our lack of specific skill sets do not disqualify us from God's desire to use us if we are willing.

the Twelve is something we should both mourn and heed. How could one who was so close to Jesus so fully miss the transformation Jesus desired to do in his life and in the world? Judas's physical proximity to Jesus somehow failed to traverse the chasm between Judas's empire imagination and Jesus's kingdom of the martyr church.

When They Say No

The church also must deal with those who walk away from discipleship and even the faith. Though it is devastating and heartbreaking, sometimes people are not ready to receive the proclamation of the gospel, for a variety of reasons. Even Jesus had people walk away. The three synoptic Gospels tell the story of a character who has come to be known in common parlance as "the rich young ruler."[1] In these accounts, this man wanted to obtain eternal life. Jesus asked about his faithfulness to Jewish law, and he affirmed he had been obedient. Jesus did not seem to doubt the man's claims of lifelong faithfulness. The man appeared genuine and authentic.

Mark 10:21 says, "Jesus looked at him carefully and loved him." In light of this loving encounter Jesus told him, "You are lacking one thing. Go, sell what you own, and give the money to the poor. Then you will have treasure in heaven. And come, follow me" (v. 21). Jesus knew the only thing this man needed in order to experience eternal life—not only in the afterlife but in this life—was to be set free from the oppression of his possessions. The man was dismayed and sad because, as Scripture notes, "he had many possessions" (v. 22). This man's love of his possessions was more than this love for Jesus and the invitation to eternal life.

---

1. This title is simply a compilation of all the Gospels. Matthew 19 notes he is young and rich. Mark 10 notes he is rich. Luke 18 calls him a rich ruler.

Sometimes in the church, the gospel message is too hard to accept.

Although we do not water down the cost of discipleship, there are important cautions. Sometimes the church has placed barriers in front of people that God never intended. Paul's great concern about circumcision in Galatians is one example of the Jewish believers making it harder for gentiles to be part of the church than God would've wanted (see Galatians 5:1–15). Moreover, some parts of the church are guilty of simply keeping people away whom the church has deemed unfit for Jesus and the kingdom. Remember the stories in Mark 10 about the disciples trying to keep children from Jesus and the crowds telling blind Bartimaeus to shut up?

What extra barriers has the church placed in front of potential disciples today?

God Calls Women to Lead the Church

Some in the church have created and continue to create a gender barrier for women in pastoral leadership. The broader Wesleyan tradition resolutely affirms that God calls women to full-time pastoral ministry service and leadership in all areas of the church. What follows is not an exhaustive argument but a beginning scriptural basis for celebrating the importance of God's calling, equipping, and celebrating women in church leadership.

We acknowledge first that all of Scripture was written in a patriarchal world. This context shapes all of Scripture, and attempts to ignore this bias are dishonest. However, within both Testaments, there are numerous accounts of women in crucial areas of leadership in the church. Within the Bible's patriarchal context, the radical approach to gender equality that is articulated and celebrated in the New Testament specifically must not be overlooked. This approach testifies both to the radical reversal of the new

Wesleyan Ecclesial Confession

We do not weaken or soften the call to discipleship in order to make it more palatable. The church must extend the gracious, rich, deep, full call of the gospel to find life by giving it all to God. To soften the call of discipleship is to water down both its cost and its gift. The call of the gospel is the road to life, but on this narrow road not all are willing to go through that crucible (Matthew 7:13–14). We are all damaged when the call to discipleship is watered down to make it more attractive to those with empire ambitions.

creation kingdom and the bravery of the women who re-sponded to God's invitation despite the avalanche of sexist bias against them.[2]

Women in the first century were often considered property—persons who had no right to speak to men publicly. Their testimony was not valid in any court of law. Their primary function was domestic in the birthing and shaping of children and maintaining an efficient home life. Women are found throughout the Gospels, starting with Mary the mother of Jesus, but the Gospels clearly celebrate and elevate the faithful presence of women specifically at the foot of the cross and then at the tomb.

The Women Disciples

John 19 notes the three Marys at the cross, setting up the dynamic scene of Jesus releasing his role as son to the disciple "whom he loved" (see John 19:26–27). Not only were the women present to Jesus at the cross, but they were also the ones who were headed to the tomb to care for Jesus's body on that first day of the week (Matthew 28:1; Mark 16:1; Luke 24:1; John 20:1).

Depending on the Gospel story, the women encoun-tered either an angel or Jesus at the tomb and were commis-sioned as the first evangelists of Jesus's resurrection. This setup was not accidental. Women's testimony at that time was not worth the paper it was written on. Yet, even while the men cowered in pity, fear, and pain, the women—de-spite their pain, heartache, and fear—found a way to Jesus's tomb to care for him. Hovey notes that, "The reliability of [the women's testimony] is disabled by their gender in that patriarchal milieu. Yet it is the women who are promised to see Jesus in Galilee, who had not abandoned Jesus at the cross, and who, Mark explains, had followed and served Je-

---

2. See Rachel Held Evans, "Who's Who Among Biblical Women Leaders," June 6, 2012, https://rachelheldevans.com/blog/mutuality-women-leaders.

sus in Galilee (15:40–41). . . . After all, a gospel proclaimed by women and uneducated fisherman is a social sign of the cosmic reversal that the gospel heralds."[3] The women were entrusted to bear the greatest and most unbelievable news that had ever been or ever will be offered.

Paul's Thoughts on Women in the Church

In Galatians, Paul affirms with kingdom clarity the equality among people of religious, economic, and gender differences (3:28). He was not violently declaring all people are the same but affirming that all people are equally beautiful and valuable because of diversity in the kingdom of God.

Sadly, 1 Corinthians 14, also written by Paul, is used today to deny women leadership roles and the space to speak in front of men in the church. While addressing numerous problems within the church at Corinth, Paul was calling for order in worship. Although the bulk of this chapter was Paul pastorally addressing how to handle speaking in tongues, he also raised an issue near the end of the chapter about order in worship: "God isn't a God of disorder but of peace. Like in all the churches of God's people, the women should be quiet during the meeting. They are not allowed to talk. Instead, they need to get under control, just as the Law says. If they want to learn something, they should ask their husbands at home. It is disgraceful for a woman to talk during the meeting" (vv. 33–35).

Many have interpreted Paul as declaring that God does not want women speaking in worship or having pastoral leadership in the church. However, a closer look at the text reveals that the women in this Corinthian congregation had many questions about their new faith and were disrupting the church service *with* their questions.

---

3. Hovey, *To Share in the Body*, 127. See also Augustine, *City of God*, 22.5.

My children and I have come to be nerds of the Marvel Universe. My daughter is relentless in following all the news and theories about the Marvel Universe. Since I am older and slower, I need a little more help. Often during a movie in the theater, I would pepper my daughter with incessant questions about the characters and plots. Finally, my daughter kindly asserted, "Dad, we can talk about this after the movie at home." My desire to learn was genuine, but my timing was not appropriate. My daughter was more than happy to enlighten me on all the twists and theories—but not during the movie. It is likely this was Paul's goal for the church in Corinth as well.

These women were asking honest questions, but it was not appropriate for them to disrupt the service, so Paul suggested they discuss their questions at home with their husbands. These verses in 1 Corinthians 14 are an example of a pastoral situation Paul addressed for *one* church. It was not a universal policy that meant to banish women from pastoral leadership. Christians must take care to discern when it is and is not appropriate to attempt a universal application of scriptural passages addressing specific contexts.

Another passage used to disqualify women from leadership in the church is from 1 Timothy 2, where Paul is giving instructions for both men and women. In verse 12, Paul admonishes that women should not teach or control husbands but rather be "a quiet listener." Many have used this passage as further confirmation that women should not lead or instruct men, which would preclude their pastoral leadership in the church. Again, Paul was addressing an issue in a local congregation. Using this passage as a universal denial of women in leadership is poor interpretation. There is no valid theological reason for women not to be leaders in the church. If it seemed good to the Holy Spirit and to Jesus to entrust women to proclaim the good news of Christ's resurrection to the disciples, then it must be good enough for us to encourage, celebrate, and elect women to leadership positions.

Not only did Paul celebrate that in the new kingdom there is equality between men and women, but he also celebrated women who were leaders in the early church. The late Rachel Held Evans notes that the apostle Junia "is perhaps the most silenced woman of the Bible."[4] In Romans 16:7, Paul indicates that Junia was an outstanding apostle. Held Evans highlights John Chrysostom's affirmation and celebration of Junia's apostleship, but a patriarchal church found her to be problematic, so her memory has largely been forgotten, and some even changed the name to a masculine Junias.[5] Still other women leaders are scattered throughout the epistles, including Phoebe in Romans 16:1–2 and Priscilla (along with her husband, Aquila) in Romans 16:3–4.

The emphasis here is not to engage in a proof-text battle over women leaders in the church. This issue is larger than mere scriptural interpretation. Even within the thick patriarchal context in which the Scriptures were written and collected, the mere presence of women leaders in both Testaments is revolutionary. Although misogynistic and patriarchal sins still exist deep into the twenty-first century, God's desire to use women to lead the martyr church is a further embodied testimony of God's new creation kingdom breaking forth.

Priesthood of All Believers

To this point the focus of the conversation has given primary attention to those called into pastoral ministry. However, all Christians can be used by God to share their

---

4. Held Evans, "Who's Who Among Biblical Women Leaders," https://rachel heldevans.com/blog/mutuality-women-leaders.

5. Held Evans also points to Scot McKnight's *Junia Is Not Alone* and Eldon Jay Epp's *Junia: The First Woman Apostle*.

faith and testimony wherever they go. God has a calling—a *vocation*—for all Christians to participate in the present and coming kingdom of God. The term "priest" does not describe any one individual in the New Testament but references the whole community: "But you are a chosen race, a royal priesthood, a holy nation, a people who are God's own possession. You have become this people so that you may speak of the wonderful acts of the one who called you out of darkness into his amazing light" (1 Peter 2:9).

This text in 1 Peter indicates that all Christians ought to continue in the priestly ministry given to Abraham and his descendants. This calling to be a light to all the nations is about testimony of what God has done and is doing in bringing us from darkness to light. This calling is not for a select few but for all. Revelation 1:6 also affirms that God has made the church "a kingdom and priests to serve his God and Father" (NIV).

While not all persons have the same gifts and part in the body, 1 Corinthians 12 affirms that every member is important. In fact, pushing against the idea that those with more public gifts of leadership are more important, Paul notes that special honor is given to those parts of the body that are less visible and often considered the weakest (see vv. 22–24). All are gifted, and those gifts are to be used for God's present and coming kingdom and not for our own personal glory. Romans 12:4–8 beautifully celebrates many gifts that are to be part of the one church.

The question is not *if* God has gifted us but whether we are willing to *come and follow*. Will we find our true vocation in accumulating wealth, fame, or possessions of empire that can be stolen and rot? Or will we make our life's call about *fishing for people* whom God has put in our stream and invited us to love with the unique gifts and passions God has given us?

Jesus invites all to *come and follow me!*

EIGHT

Laity and Clergy in the Church

Chapter 7 concluded by celebrating that God invites all Christians to be ministers of the gospel as part of the priesthood of all believers (1 Peter 2:9), a foundational tenet of the Protestant tradition. God invites all Christians to come and follow Christ and make their life's pursuit about seeking first God's kingdom and righteousness (Matthew 6:33). God chose Abraham and his descendants to be a blessing to *all* the nations of the world by reflecting Yahweh's image and inviting others into this covenant of love (Genesis 12:3).

From Abraham to Isaac to Jacob, there were bumps along the way. Not only testifying to others about the way of Yahweh but even loving their own family proved challenging. From Jacob, the twelve tribes came forth. After four hundred years (ten generations) of bondage in Egypt, Moses led them out through the Red Sea.

Although all twelve tribes were expected to live into the Abrahamic covenant in testifying to the way of Yahweh as a blessing to all the nations, God raised up the tribe of Levi specifically for priestly leadership within the Israelites (Deuteronomy 10:8–9). The Levites were tasked with the administration of the tabernacle worship space and the rituals of the Israelites from the wilderness into the promised land, carrying on the ministry of Aaron (Numbers 1:48–53).[1]

All the Israelites were God's chosen people. All tribes crossed the Red Sea and emerged (baptized) out of death to new life. The Levites were still Israelites, but they had a specialized calling. Similarly, all clergy and pastors are Christians but have been given a unique gifting and equipping. For the contemporary church, two important terms help clarify this relationship: *laity* and *clergy*. Unfortunately, too often these terms have been used to divide "average" Christians from the leaders of the church. This distinction is neither helpful nor true. Just as Levites were first Israelites, clergy are first and foremost Christians in the martyr church.

Sadly, as the church matured and gained more prominence and power, a marked distinction between clergy and laity developed that is today long and multi-faceted. One aspect of the division is the professionalization of ministry, which encourages all Christians to participate in worship and live exemplary lives, but only the paid pastor is expected to share the good news, visit the sick and poor, care for the homeless, evangelize, and lead the church in worship and administration. Some Christians think paying their tithe is their ticket out of certain Christian duties. This mindset is unfortunate because one of the primary responsibilities of a pastor is to encourage, equip, and train Christians to experience God's transforming love and live out that love in the world as a minister of God's hope and grace. God desires to empower *every* Christian to share the good news of what God has done in our lives in our own style and way. First Peter exhorts all Christians to be ready to share their faith with humility, kindness, and hospitality (3:15–17).

---

1. Numbers 3, 4, 8, and 18 detail further the specific call and responsibility of the Levites.

Ordained as Laity at Baptism

The term "ordination" is often connected with Christians who are clergy—those given pastoral, or priestly, leadership in the church. This association is correct, but all persons become most fully Christian at their baptism, which celebrates a person's initiation into the church, the body of Christ. At baptism all Christians are *ordained* into the ministry of the *laity*. Hence, all laity are ordained to be ministers of the gospel (priesthood of all believers). As ordained, laity are set apart and consecrated as Christians to become part of God's holy people, used by God as part of the renewal and redemption of all things.

Karl Barth emphasized the great gift of baptism awakening the knowledge of Jesus Christ and the power of the Holy Spirit, but there is more: "The task of every Christian—not additionally but from the very outset, on every step of the way assigned to him in baptism—is his task as a bearer of the gospel to the others who still stand without."[2] For Barth, the encounter with Christ and the Spirit at baptism immediately obligates the baptized to share the gospel in the world, and these marching orders come in light of the Great Commission in Matthew 28. The great danger that Barth pushes against is that the ordination of clergy may begin to creep into the ordination of the laity as articulated in the Great Commission (Matthew 28:19). Those ordained as clergy never lose their ordination as laity conferred at baptism. In fact, the unique charisma and/or gifts and authority given upon clerical ordination are largely for leadership in the church and specifically for communal worship. Barth also helps summarize the key focus and

---

2. Karl Barth, "Baptism with Water," *Church Dogmatics Vol IV.4: The Doctrine of Reconciliation,* eds. G. W. Bromiley and T. F. Torrance (Peabody, MA: Hendrickson, 2010), 200.

calling of the ordination of clergy as *a servant to the servants of God.*[3]

The *Manual* of the Church of the Nazarene states about ministry and Christian service, "The Church of the Nazarene recognizes all believers are called to minister to all people."[4] Moreover, when it goes on to parse the "Categories of Ministry," it begins with lay ministry, an intentional acknowledgment that all laity are to be ministers in the world.[5] All Christians, ordained at baptism as laity, are given a vocation to minister in the world with the gifts God has given us. The temptation is to use those gifts and talents given by God for empire kingdom and not for the kingdom of God that is here now and still more fully coming.

Laity Called to Be Clergy

Just as all Christians are called to be ministers of Christ's love and forgiveness, God calls and equips some from the laity for additional leadership in the church. These pastors have a unique calling of leading the church in communal worship and equipping the rest of the body to fulfill their calling to be Christ's body and blood in the world. There is a distinction of gifts and responsibilities between those who are ordained as laity and those from the laity who are also ordained as pastors and bishops in the church. Above all, even as some pastors are given unique leadership responsibilities, there is equality among God's holy people.

The union between Christ and the church is the primary form of relationship between Christian sisters and brothers. Morris Pelzel offers an example of this primary union among baptized Christians between laity and clergy: "A layperson in the church meets and relates to his or her

---

3. Barth, *Church Dogmatics IV.4*, 201.

4. Church of the Nazarene, *Manual*, 192.

5. Church of the Nazarene, *Manual*, 194–95.

pastor first as a fellow Christian and secondly as an ordained priest."[6] This way of relating first celebrates a united and equal union in Christ. Augustine further expounds on the unique relationship between laity and clergy: "What I am *for* you terrifies me; what I am *with* you consoles me. For you I am a bishop; but with you I am a Christian. The former is a duty, the latter a grace. The former is a danger; the latter, salvation."[7] Augustine's words are a beautiful prayer of the dynamic relationship between laity and clergy. This first communion in God allows for the order of the church in which some of the ordained laity are also ordained as clergy for equipping all Christians and leading the church in communal worship.

Clergy: Servants of the Servants of God

Servus servorum Dei ("servant of the servants of God") is a phrase with a long history in Christianity. It is likely to have originated in Roman Catholicism and was often used only to describe popes.[8] However, it feels appropriate for all clergy to see how the gifts and authority offered at clerical ordination are all about serving Christians and equipping them to fulfill their calling as ministers of the gospel in their daily lives.

Ephesians 4 offers helpful instruction. Paul told the church in Ephesus that God has raised up leaders in order that all Christians may live in unity and faith. Moreover, the clergy are to work by the power of the Spirit to help the

---

6. Morris Pelzel, *Ecclesiology: The Church as Communion and Mission* (Chicago: Loyola Press, 2001), 14.

7. Augustine of Hippo, "Sermon 340," cited in *Lumen Gentium #32*, 1, emphasis added.

8. The *Catholic Encyclopedia* notes that Pope Gregory the Great was the first pope to use the phrase *servus servorum Dei* regularly. Gregory believed the phrase helped him see his role of pope as one of humble servanthood (Andrew Meehan, "*Servus sevorum Dei*," *The Catholic Encyclopedia* Vol. 13 (New York: Robert Appleton Company, 1912), http://www.newadvent.org/cathen/13737a.htm.

church grow and mature into Christ, who is the head of the church. Each Christian grows together in love, living into the unique gifts we have been given (see vv. 11–15). The clergy's calling is to equip God's people—not for easy, safe, comfortable lives but for work and service, being used by God for the present and coming kingdom.

This unity in love is not uniformity but rather celebrates the beautiful diversity of God's creation. This unity in faith invites the church to move onto maturity as persons are more fully transformed into the image of Jesus Christ. For Wesleyans this transformation is the healing of sanctification. In Ephesus, and for the church broadly, this maturity involved being grounded in Jesus and not easily fooled, manipulated, or paranoid.

For the church in the twenty-first century, Christians are too often tossed back and forth by fear. One primary fear arises around those who are not like us, which leads to all kinds of mistreatment, misunderstanding, bigotry, isolation, and often violence. Rather, if Christians mature into Christ, we will become prisoners of hope (see Zechariah 9:12). The kryptonite to fear is hope.

Hope is not naïve, ignorant, wishful thinking. Grounded in the love of the triune God and the power of Jesus Christ's death and resurrection, the church in its maturity is set free from enslavement to sin, fear, and death. The calling of clergy is to be a conduit of God's grace in order that Christians may mature in love and the hope and power of Jesus Christ, and find our work and service in the world as part of God's healing and renewal of all things.

Also noteworthy in the Ephesians text is the number of ministry roles listed. Paul names apostles, prophets, evangelists, pastors, and teachers. Historically in Christian tradition there has not been a uniformity in titles of clerical offices.[9] Though there are some discernible structures in the New Testament, most scholars agree that "there was no fixed pattern of leadership in the first century."[10] The designations they did use are a window into the very young church that was still working out the structure and often doing so in the face of persecution.

Process of Ordaining Clergy

With the strong emphasis that all Christians are ordained as laity at baptism, there is still the important role of ordaining lay members into the pastoral office as deacons, elders, and bishops and/or superintendents. The process varies by denomination, though there are often overlapping commonalities. In the Church of the Nazarene when a person feels called to ministry, they must first receive a local license from their own church board. After a minimum of one year, with the blessing and affirmation of the local church, they can then apply for a district license. During this process, the candidate will be working on a course of study for ministerial preparation. After a set number of years of service and with annual district interviews and completed educational requirements, the district can then recommend that a candidate be ordained by the overseeing general superintendent.[11] It must be celebrated that there is testimony of calling and gifting by the individual, the local church, the district, and general leadership. My declaration that God has called me to be a pastor can be

---

9. The Church of the Nazarene celebrates that each local church is unique and part of the whole: "The church is a historical reality that organizes itself in culturally conditioned forms, exists both as local congregations and as a universal body, and also sets apart persons called of God for specific ministries (*Manual*, 33).

10. W. T. Purkiser, Richard S. Taylor, and Willard H. Taylor, *God, Man, & Salvation: A Biblical Theology* (Kansas City, MO: Beacon Hill Press of Kansas City, 1977), 602.

11. See Church of the Nazarene, *Manual*, paragraph 534.3, pp. 219–20.

honest and sincere. Yet my calling must also be affirmed by the larger church body.

In addition to God's call, part of God's equipping includes proper teaching and training in the faith through formal education. The apostle Paul repeatedly talked about how he was passing on what he had received (see 1 Corinthians 11:23; 15:3). Through Christian history it has been crucial that leaders in the church faithfully know and proclaim the faith. In the New Testament and earliest iterations of the church, faithful proclamation was known as *kerygma.* Although elders are charged to proclaim the gospel in their unique context, there are parts of the Christian *kerygma* ("proclamation," "teaching," "doctrine") that are not to be dismantled or changed.

Paul experienced several intense aspects of his training and education. In Acts 22:3 we learn that he studied under Gamaliel, a highly respected Jewish rabbi. Galatians 1:12 reports the powerful revelation of the gospel from Jesus Christ to Paul. Paul received this revelation and also spent time with the apostles. Paul provides a helpful model that, although God can encounter each person, part of one's preparation for ministry involves formation through education. Formative education is not simply about being able to recall facts, figures, and precise chronology. It is about transformation as well as trust that one will faithfully proclaim the Christian *kerygma.*

The Solemn Act of Clerical Ordination

Laity who are called to full-time administrative and communal worship leadership in the church are ordained as clergy. Some parts of Roman Catholic and Orthodox Christianity celebrate the ordination of elders and deacons as an official sacrament. Even though most Protestant denominations do not name ordination as a sacrament, most all traditions hold the ordination of clergy as holy and sacred. The journey of discernment of one's calling, gifts, and graces for ministry, and the competence to faithfully live and proclaim the Christian *kerygma* is significant. At the appointed time the church will gather to ordain persons into the role of elder or deacon.

The process of ordination is twofold. First, ordination is an act of affirmation that one is called, gifted, graced, and faithfully able to proclaim the gospel. Second, ordination is an act whereby the Spirit offers unique and powerful gifts for the person to faithfully embody the ministries to which they are charged. In this sense, ordained clergy are empowered, equipped, and authorized to offer leadership in the church that others are not. Discerning gifts for local ministry is not about some being more valuable but all working together by the Spirit.

The Church of the Nazarene celebrates two offices of clergy, elder and deacon. Both share leadership in the church, but the elder is distinctly called and empowered for preaching and the administration of sacraments, while the deacon is called as a helping minister of support for a local church.[12] As clergy members, pastors can also be called and blessed to be district and general superintendents. There is not a new ordination, but in these roles a new commission for specific leadership in the church is given.

Conclusion

God invites all Christians to see their lives as called by God. This calling is not a matter of where one's paycheck comes from; all Christians are called to share and proclaim the good news of the Gospel regardless of their contexts. In addition, some Christians are called for specific leadership in the church. Those ordained as deacons, elders, and then

---

12. See Church of the Nazarene, *Manual*, 217–20.

bishops and/or superintendents are given specific roles and gifts of service in the body of Christ.

Those who are called to lead are to be *the servants of the servants of God.* The key is not about competition but celebrating God's desire to use and partner with human beings to participate in God's further healing and redeeming of all creation.

NINE

Healthy Leadership in the Martyr Church

How does the martyr church live into its calling? Before discussing the importance of covenant and order, the martyr church lives out of a distinct goal and purpose. Most institutions (governments, universities, corporations, news media, etc.) have one primary goal: do not die! Hence, raw pragmatism becomes the central mission that guides most decisions at a basic level. Missional pragmatism is the way of empire. Sadly, churches can also be seduced into making decisions out of the fear of death. Yet, while the martyr church never seeks to die, it does seek to be faithful to God even if that means it will cease to exist in this life. The martyr church refuses the raw pragmatism of empire that *we must survive at all costs.* Refusing to sacrifice everything on the altar of pragmatism and/or survival is a call for costly faithfulness to God, not a celebration or encouragement of poor judgment. Polity and leadership in a local church ought to be embodied through the lens of the martyr church.

Polity in the Church

Similar to the roles of clergy, we don't have a robust biblical example to follow when it comes to church administration. The Scriptures certainly provide the fullness of the gospel in every way that is necessary for salvation, but we must acknowledge that these texts have captured the early church in its administrative infancy and immaturity. That is why we are grateful for the gift of church history and tradition. Although the Protestant Reformation sought to challenge some practices of the Catholic Church that were inappropriate, the Reformation also celebrated the role of Scripture alongside the church's great and guiding tradition.

Throughout Scripture God keeps bringing order out of chaos. From Genesis 1 all the way to Pentecost in Acts 2, God finds beauty in the ordering of creation from sin (chaos) to best reflect God's image (shalom). This celebration of order does not mean Christians should not be part of revolutions against empires that practice injustice and oppression. To make sure you saw that double negative it can also be said, Christians *should* work against sinful powers and principalities of chaos. Such revolutions participate in God's further inbreaking of the new creation on earth as it is in heaven.

In light of this blessing of God's order, the local church should also work to be faithful to a consistent order of organization, often called "polity." A church's polity is a gift to help minimize chaos. While all structures can become idols if we are not careful and open to adaptation, polity can help guide denominations and local churches. Many denominations have codified their polity in written documents that have guided them throughout history. The Church of the Nazarene calls its polity document the *Manual,* while the United Methodists have the *Book of Discipline* and *Book of Worship* to guide them. Other denominations and traditions have their own documents as well. Typically these documents are open to change and contextual adjustment as Christians within our institutions seek to faithfully embody Christ in the world. Change for an entire denomination is often difficult and slow because of the need to consult members all over the globe who deserve to weigh in. On the other hand, local churches can run into significant legal and theological problems when pastors ignore polity details and seek to run their local church as they see fit.

Many denominations organize groups of local churches into larger geographical districts that are overseen by an administrator. "District superintendent" is a common title for this administrative role, but it is not the only title. Most of the time, administrative leaders who preside over a group of multiple local churches are clergy who have previously served as local pastors themselves. Although there is no perfect structure, there are a few encouragements for local churches and pastors who serve within a denomination or tradition that has a specific polity structure already in place.

1. Know the polity. Both legal problems and unnecessary conflicts can arise in a local church when boards, councils, administrative teams, and/or pastors are ignorant of or intentionally disregard what the tradition or institution has already laid out as policy.

2. View the polity as a gift. While the demands upon a local pastor and leaders in a church are exponential, having some structure already in place can save a great deal of time and prevent conflict by simply following what the larger denomination has already affirmed.

3. Stay open to revising the polity. No church structure is perfect; therefore, most denominations have mechanisms and procedures in place whereby members, leaders, clergy, and groups can recommend or propose changes to statements of belief or organizational governance. Revisions are not easy and generally require a certain percentage of agreement from representatives across the whole of a denomination. Many denominations convene periodic conferences, meetings, or assemblies for the express purpose of considering proposed changes and recommendations. Such action takes time, dialogue, grace, and a great deal of work.

My pastor and friend Scott Daniels recalled a conversation he had with a pastor friend from a nondenominational church. As Scott was discussing the process for making denominational polity changes, his friend asked, "Does it bother you to belong to a church that votes on its theology?"

Scott replied, "Does it bother you that you belong to a church that just made up its theology?"

Governance books offer guidelines and safety nets that can and should be changed when it is contextually appropriate. It has never impressed me when local pastors simply decide they know best and cast off their denomination's polity documents because they find it too constricting. While there is usually room for appropriate contextual adaptation, many local churches and pastors have lost their way because they failed to discipline themselves to their overarching tradition's organization.

4. Consider the polity a covenant among Christians. Persons who enter into membership in a local church that is tied to a larger tradition or institution voluntarily submit themselves to that organization's polity. Moreover, pastors who are ordained in a denomination also pledge to live under the discipline of that tradition. Submission to discipline is best imagined as joining a uniquely covenanted people as part of the larger universal church.

It may be helpful to draw upon the timeless wisdom of the character Barbossa from Disney's *Pirates of the Caribbean*. When speaking about the code of the pirate's brethren to Elizabeth Swann, who attempts to claim fair treatment from the code, Barbossa extols, "You must be a pirate for the pirate's code to apply, and you're not. And the code is more what you'd call 'guidelines' than actual rules." Of course, church polity documents are usually more binding than that, but the overall goal is to help enhance and facilitate the ministry of a local church, not to be an overwhelming burden. Wisdom can also be found by consulting one's administrative overseers (the district superintendents) and even other, more experienced pastors when navigating administration and polity questions.

The Danger of Board Shaping

I come from a long line of dedicated laity. While Christianity is wide and deep on both sides of my family, there have been few clergy. Even so, my laity family members have been active, opinionated, and vocal in their churches. One of the joys of my father's life as a layperson was the honor and duty of serving on church boards for more than forty years. When I become a pastor his wisdom and counsel were helpful in my ministry. One area that concerns us greatly is related to the danger of intentionally shaping a board in order to accomplish a specific purpose.

Most denominations provide guidance for how local church boards or administrative councils should be elected. I have seen pastors either manipulate the guidelines or just not use them. These pastors are often weak leaders who want to plant people on the board who will not go against their ideas. This unacceptable practice is often rooted in fear and the way of empire. While people who are obstinate just to create chaos are not helpful, a strong church board will have persons represented from a wide cross-section of the congregation and should comprise people who are not afraid to speak up in disagreement but who also can be gracious when the majority makes a final decision.

One place where pastors and nominating committees *should* work with intentionality to shape boards and administrative councils regards diversity. Strong church boards are not only willing to ask hard questions but are also diverse in regard to gender, ethnicity, socioeconomic status, age, and perhaps other categories.

Servant Leadership

Here are a few words of encouragement for pastors and local congregations.

Wesleyan Ecclesial Confession

One of the greatest leadership and life lessons comes from Proverbs 27:6. "Well meant are the wounds a friend inflicts, but profuse are the kisses of an enemy" (NRSVUE). Weak leaders surround themselves with people who simply agree and do not challenge their leadership decisions. Such leaders often create a world where the emperor has on no clothes yet no one is willing to say so. Conversely, the Wesleyan tradition has a long history of elevating leaders who desire competent, diverse perspectives that empower and encourage disagreement and challenge with troublesome ideas.

First, *all pastors are interim.* One of the great blessings in my lifetime among many denominations is that pastoral assignments are lengthening. It has been my experience that the longer a pastor's tenure at a local church, the more the pastor and people can grow in health as a local body and the greater the missional impact in their community will be. My assertion that all pastors are interim is not about length of ministry but about how each pastor must recognize it is not "her" or "his" church but God's church that we are called to steward and lead. As pastors think about their role, it is good to remember that each church has a history that must be cherished (even new church plants!). Respecting this reality does not mean all history is good and needs to be preserved, but arriving pastors must recognize and honor the people and history that have brought the church to this point.[1] As pastors and lay leaders work together, pastors must establish layers of trust, and moving slower is usually best.

Second, *the decision-making process is often more important than the decisions that are made.* I am a decisive person and not a fan of lingering. While I do not make rash decisions, I like to act in a timely manner. However, as a leader I must learn to respect my team so that some key decisions can be made together. Team decisions take longer. The process for how the decision is made is as important as, if not more than, the actual decision. A key part of any decision is communication. Over-communicating and over-listening are rare. Pastors should listen long and deep. I can attest to the notions of *death by committee* and *analysis paralysis.* A robust tension between efficiency and thoughtful engagement with lay leaders and the broader congregation is essential.

1. A great resource for pastors and lay leaders especially in navigating the beginning of a relationship is: T. Scott Daniels, *The First 100* Days: *A Pastor's Guide* (Kansas City, MO: Beacon Hill Press of Kansas City, 2011).

Jesse Middendorf asserts that change will happen more slowly in local churches (and take even longer perhaps in small churches) than in other organizations. He suggests that *telling time* is essential in the process of making decisions. Telling time is not simply the chronological time of the hour, day, or year, but in the Spirit of Acts 2 the *kairotic* (seasonally or emotionally or circumstantially appropriate) time for making good decisions.[2] Patience is a virtue that good leaders develop. Leaders must not offer too much change too quickly. There must be adequate time for persons to properly absorb the rate of change.[3] Too much too fast will likely not be helpful. I have numerous times seen pastors and church leaders make excellent decisions via toxic processes, rendering the benefits irrelevant. Church leaders must always pay attention to the difference between the seductions of empire and the invitation of the martyr church.

Third, *change is often experienced as relational loss.* When the COVID-19 pandemic began in 2020, the world experienced change in ways that had not been seen in decades, if ever. Local churches were certainly impacted in many ways, most notably in our forced transition to online-only church for at least a few weeks. This hardship allowed the global church to reflect on its very nature, bringing important ideas to the forefront of the dialogue, including the notions that we do not *go* to church—we *are* the church, and that the church is never closed but always open for the Spirit to dwell among God's people. Even so, there was still tremendous loss that it became crucial to name. The decision in

---

2. Jesse Middendorf, "The Sociology of the Small Church during and after the COVID Season." Seminar given at Physically Distant and Relationally Strong seminar series, Northwest Nazarene University (Nampa, ID), July 7, 2020, https://www.youtube.com/watch?v=FMhUpX6De7w.

3. See Tod Bolsinger, *Canoeing the Mountains: Christian Leadership in Uncharted Territory* (Downers Grove, IL: InterVarsity Press, 2015), 123.

2020 to close church buildings was difficult, but it was a result of external forces; there are other difficult decisions that have to be made as a result of internal forces.

I have been blessed in my life to serve with wonderful pastors in local churches that had amazing lay leaders. It has generally been my experience that pastors have been more interested in initiating change than lay leaders. The laity often seek to conserve or preserve norms, while pastors tend to want to try new things (of course, the opposite also occurs). Neither posture is inherently right or wrong. There have been many times when new ideas were disastrous or when stagnation and preservation have killed churches. Conversely, I have also seen churches become transformed by new ideas while strengthening many established traditions or programs. The key is that pastors and lay leaders together keep evaluating what they do and why, and not be afraid to ask questions about how any practice, plan, or ministry is faithful to the larger kingdom of God and to the contextualized mission of that local church. Middendorf also notes that small churches live not through the completion of tasks but on the foundation of relationships. Beyond the new activity or event, the threat of change can often result in relational imbalance.[4]

Fourth, *carefully and prayerfully never waste a crisis.* No one ever wants or seeks a crisis; however, life happens, and crises will come. The COVID-19 pandemic was extremely difficult but created opportunities to ask questions and potentially take actions that may not have been considered if 2020 had been less chaotic. For example, some local churches had already set up online giving prior to 2020, and many others had discussed it but not implemented it yet. But when local churches had to stop gathering physi-

---

4. Middendorf, "The Sociology of the Small Church during and after the COVID Season."

cally due to the pandemic, it was amazing how fast nearly all churches set up a way to give online. A year or more of committee meetings and countless emails were skipped simply out of necessity. Many pastors reported that members were faithful to mail in their tithes or drop them off at the church, but many more found online giving to be a helpful tool.

Crisis periods also demonstrate a church's resilience. A friend noted that if anyone questions the resilience of an established small church, they should go ahead and try to shut that church down. The people, against all odds, will often do everything they can to keep the doors of a local congregation open.

Although crisis offers us the space to make changes, care must be taken not to manipulate circumstances or people's fear, or to take unethical advantage of opportunities that arise during crisis. Crises are great times to engage in conversations that are often thought too delicate, and they are good times to implement healthy changes.

Fifth, *when the people resist the pastor's ideas, it is likely more about loss than personal rejection.* A healthy local church board represents a dynamic cross-section of the congregation. A good board member is not obstinate or critical for the sake of being such, but healthy board members ask hard questions. When lay members oppose pastoral ideas, pastors should remember that such opposition is almost always about ideas and not about the pastor personally. Yes, there are those who will make it personal, but most invested laity who challenge ideas are actually showing their love and support for the local church and the pastor by raising their concerns. Those who oppose the most strongly likely perceive themselves as having the most to lose relationally. Insecure pastors may make the mistake of conflating their ideas with their identity, thereby interpreting any challenge or opposition as a personal affront to their ministry.

Sixth, *the lead pastor needs to keep the coolest temperature in the room.* Pastors can easily become frustrated when things are not going their way. A pastor must always remain calm, especially when those around them become heated or emotional. Healthy leadership teams create a safe space for honest, loving disagreement. Pastors must remain calm in order to help make sure that discussions stay productive and on track. If the pastor becomes too emotionally involved, they may have a hard time seeing clearly when the conversation needs to be redirected or paused. Pastors must work to maintain a healthy room temperature with an atmosphere of safety and listening.[5]

Seventh, *all should be nervous when God's will and a dominant leader's personal preferences are magically aligned.* One dangerous tactic a pastor or any church leader can employ is the notion that their personal preferences are also the will of God. For example, a pastor once said to a board, "God told me that God prefers X musical style for our worship service." It was beyond coincidental that X musical style happened to also be the pastor's personally preferred style. Seeking God's will is essential, but God speaks and confirms in community, not just through one voice—not even the pastor's. Moreover, God does not prefer one musical style over another. Claiming otherwise is an empire trait of spiritual manipulation.

Eighth, *a pastor must lead with grace and humility and a sense of humor.* Servant leadership has been recognized in Christian circles and beyond as a wonderful posture of leadership. As part of servant leadership, a pastor must be aware of the power dynamics at work in a local congregation. A pastor must work to lead with humility and serve

---

5. See Ronald Heifetz, Alexander Grashow, and Marty Linsky, *The Practice of Adaptive Leadership: Tools and Tactics for Changing Your Organization and the World* (Harvard Business Press, 2009), 107–08.

the people. Service does not mean being a doormat but one who actively loves others and seeks their healing and flourishing love. A pastor must keep working hard to listen and learn from others. A pastor wins when people in their congregation feel loved, equipped, and empowered. Losing is when, for the sake of being "right," people feel ignored, abused, or demeaned.

To lead with humility does not mean a pastor cannot love a person by challenging and even admonishing a person's actions. Pastors should apologize when people feel hurt, even when the pastor did not mean to hurt another (and especially if the pastor did mean to hurt). Apologizing for how a pastor's actions were received is important. Saying, "I am sorry," even when a pastor did not intend any harm, is good practice. Pastors should realize that sometimes anger directed toward the pastor is rooted in other areas of a church member's life. Humble and authentic apologies can create a space to pastorally explore other areas in a person's life. However, sometimes anger and intense frustration are a direct result of a pastor's actions; hence, discernment is crucial. Leading in humility and love is the way of the martyr church.

Adaptive Leadership

David Bowser introduced me to the field of adaptive leadership.[6] In leadership there is a tension between surviving in maintenance mode or thriving in missional living. The idea is not that it's a binary choice but a healthy balance Bowser labeled "sur-thriving."[7] Bowser suggested

---

6. Dr. Bowser recommended a few resources he has found helpful: *Leadership on the Line*, by Ronald Heifetz and Marty Linsky; *Canoeing the Mountains*, by Tod Bolsinger; and *A Failure of Nerve*, by Edwin H. Friedman.

7. These notes emerge from David Bowser's session "Adaptive Leadership" at NNU's Physically Distant and Relationally Strong seminar series, July 14, 2020, https://youtu.be/LDsPUOp0aCs.

one of the key ways to sur-thrive is discerning which types of challenges need attention. He says most challenges are either *technical* or *adaptive*.

Some examples from the COVID-19 pandemic can help clarify the differences. A church not knowing how to stream the worship service on Facebook is a *technical* challenge that requires someone with expertise. A church deciding whether to allow people in the building and whether to require or encourage masks are *adaptive* challenges. The technical challenge looks for a single expert in the room, while the adaptive challenge requires the minds of everyone present, led by the Spirit. Technical challenges look to experts or authorities to apply existing knowledge to solve a problem. Adaptive challenges invite the entire team to learn new ways and chart new paths by listening to all voices in the room.

Discerning the type of challenge is essential. The COVID-19 pandemic required both technical and adaptive leadership, which meant that discerning the type of challenges we were facing was crucial. If a room full of voices is asked to respond to a technical challenge, the result will likely be frustration and a bad outcome; often the expert's wisdom is lost in a sea of opinions. Similarly, expecting one person to solve an adaptive challenge alone is not advisable. No matter any one individual's personal expertise, adaptive challenges require a group of leaders for discernment.

Bowser also recognizes that within adaptive challenges we must pay attention to how much we can know about a situation and how well we can predict the outcome of our actions. Let's consider again a challenge from the COVID-19 pandemic. At some point every local church faced the question of when it was time to open the building doors to resume in-person worship. The multiplicity of factors each local congregation faced in this adaptive challenge was potentially overwhelming. Every church had to consider for their own context: What is the community transmission rate right now? What have the local or state governments recommended? What do health professionals recommend? If we gather, how can we do it safely? What about masks? What about singing? Should we limit how many people will be allowed inside the building at one time? And on and on. Pastors are always making decisions; drawing upon a large group of voices and experts is essential.

Pastoral leadership relies deeply on the power and wisdom of the Holy Spirit. Being a leader is hard, and being a pastoral leader is no exception. As pastors lead, we must draw on a deep well of God's love and grace. As we feel love from God, we will be better able to love the people God has entrusted us to steward. While we must continue to be dynamic preachers and teachers, we must also discipline ourselves to grow in leadership skills. We must resist leading with empire-based fear and instead lean with humility into the prophetic boldness of the martyr church. Leading well is a crucial task of the pastoral office. Moreover, a good leader will look for help leading while also cultivating an atmosphere to equip and empower new leaders. Servant leaders seek multiple perspectives in navigating the road ahead. The goal of love must never be lost. Our goal is not about being *the* leader in charge. Our goal is to allow the Holy Spirit to use us to invite persons into a deeper healing of transforming love. The calling is to prophetically call ourselves and our people to be the faithful body of the crucified and resurrected Christ. May God help us all!

Conflict in the Martyr Church

TEN

Following a covenantal polity can help local churches remain focused on their primary mission of participating in God's bringing of the new creation, and hopefully curb some conflict. However, the only local church that will be completely free of conflict is the local church without any people. In the twenty-first century, there are places on the globe where Christians are being persecuted by non-Christians, but in the United States and Europe, it appears that the largest source of the maltreatment of Christians comes from other Christians. Historically, the church has often done a terrible job dealing with conflict, both internally and externally. Scripture and other sources can guide the church in navigating and resolving conflict. While a posture of love as a gift of the Spirit is key, another powerful aid is a robust, thoughtful, contextual polity that can provide structure and order. First let's consider conflict and reconciliation with the guidance of Scripture and then outline how polity in the church is a gift from God.

Living in the joyous reality of Pentecost and the Acts 2 expression of the church did not save the early church from conflict. Scripture articulates intense levels of external persecution while also recording internal conflicts, showing us that even with the full outpouring of the Spirit, there

Wesleyan Ecclesial Confession

Conflict between humans is inevitable, even in the church. When it happens, we should allow the Spirit to help us work through it and not become stuck by it. When Christians do not have a healthy process for addressing conflict, we might be tempted to become passive-aggressive in our approach to resolution. Acting in a passive-aggressive way is not Christlike or Spirit-led. Although the dynamics and context of each situation will be different, the key is to find healthy ways to move past disagreements when they arise. Jesus did not say Christians would be known by their lack of conflict. He said, "This is how everyone will know that you are my disciples, when you love each other" (John 13:35). We do not love because we are free from conflict; we love in the midst of conflict.

will be occasions when disagreement and conflict emerge. This reality does not necessarily mean sin is present. How Christians respond to conflict is the place for attention, reflection, and in some cases confession.

One of the most notable conflicts in the New Testament is between two of the most prominent leaders in the early church: Peter and Paul. The incident is recorded in several places, most keenly in Galatians 2:11–14, which shares about the conflict from Paul's perspective. Paul was angry that Jewish Christians were telling gentile Christians they must start following Jewish laws as part of their Christian faith—specifically the need to be circumcised. In Galatians 2, Paul says Peter had been eating with gentiles up until some influential Jews came from Jerusalem. Around them, Peter refused to eat with gentiles. Paul was frustrated not only with Peter's hypocrisy but also with the fact that Peter's actions were influencing Barnabas to act the same way. In verse 14 Paul says plainly that he confronted Peter "in front of everyone." He admonished Peter to remember that people come to faithfulness through Jesus, not through Jewish Law. Paul does not tell us how Peter responded to being called out publicly. Paul's concern was not only for Peter but also for the Galatian church. We know that the confrontation between Paul and Peter was not the first time Peter experienced something like this because we remember that Jesus used a direct and public approach with Peter on multiple occasions.

The best scriptural teaching on conflict resolution and reconciliation comes from Jesus in Matthew 18. Jesus is not simply dealing with disagreement but speaks about what to do if a brother or sister sins against us. Disagreements are not necessarily sinful, but if sin is best imagined as broken relationships, then harm can occur in conflict.

Wesleyan Ecclesial Confession

Paul did not go behind Peter's back but approached him directly. Acts 15 records the breakup of Barnabas and Paul regarding John Mark. Barnabas wanted to take him, but Paul was insistent he not go after deserting them in Pamphylia (v. 38). The disagreement was so intense that Paul and Barnabas split company over it (v. 39). Acts does not share an opinion on who was "right." Paul had good reason to be concerned about John Mark, and Barnabas wanted to offer the grace of a second chance. No Christian tradition has ever been immune to conflict, and sometimes Christians must agree to disagree—but we must still love.

Jesus Lesson on Conflict #1:
Approach Directly but Privately

*If your brother or sister sins against you, go and correct them
when you are alone together. If they listen to you, then you've
won over your brother or sister. (Matthew 18:15)*

For various reasons, we Christians seem to fail to follow Jesus's advice on this point. Power dynamics may make
this first one-on-one conversation difficult. In general,
however, we often seem to find it easier to gossip or share
our frustrations with others instead of going directly to
those with whom conflict has arisen. Moreover, many times
when we find ourselves sharing offenses about someone
else, we are not the directly wronged party but are passing
on information we've heard from or about someone else.
As both a pastor and professor, I've been the subject of this
kind of indirect version of conflict:

"Did you hear what Dr. Peterson believes about . . ."

"I can't believe Rev. Peterson was so mean to . . ."

*"I would never send my kid to that corrupt religion depart-
ment, I heard they teach . . ."*

It goes on and on and on and on. On rare occasions
people have actually come to me about certain issues, but
that hasn't been the norm. Jesus makes it clear in Matthew
18:15 that gossiping to others about conflict instead of
approaching our brother or sister directly and privately is
sin. Recognizing that more often than not there are power
dynamics at play between any two humans, before we obey
Jesus's instruction to talk one on one, it may be helpful to
consult a third party—not with the motivation to gossip
but to help develop some perspective and maybe even a
strategy for dealing with the conflict. Motivation is key. Am
I talking to another person to help move toward reconciliation, or am I in conversation to prove how right I am and

how wrong the other person is? These situations require thoughtful, honest reflection.

Above all, we must be welcoming. I have had times in my life when my own insecurity caused me to be overtly defensive and unapproachable. With God's help, I want to be someone whom people feel safe bringing concerns to, even if their concerns are about me. In both my pastoral and educational roles, I talk with people all the time about subjects on which there is not complete agreement. On a few occasions, I have felt the Holy Spirit encourage me to reach out to people following my interactions with them. As I have matured and tried to follow the Spirit's prompting, I have learned several times that I caused hurt or confusion without meaning to. Other times when I've reached out, people have expressed that they weren't bothered in the least by our conversation or my words, but they are always thankful that I have circled back to check in. Being approachable and resisting the temptation to defensiveness should be part of our ongoing maturity in Christ, our growth in sanctifying grace.

Some people really struggle with guilt and finding their voice. I have served on several boards and committees with a particular pastoral colleague who is bright, wise, funny, and a joy to be with. On several occasions she has emailed me after a meeting asking if her voice was too strong. I've always told her that her tone is helpful and her comments appropriate. I slowly learned that in her past she experienced some wounds that caused her to not value her own voice and to feel guilty or insecure whenever she expressed herself in a strong way. For people in this kind of space who are prone to false guilt or are afraid to speak up, it is important to develop healthy relationships where they are encouraged and empowered to use their voice.

Each conflict is contextual and unique. In Matthew 18, Jesus is specifically referring to situations when "your

Wesleyan Ecclesial Confession

While Jesus's teaching is to be celebrated, there are some contexts where it would not be wise, advisable, or safe for those who have been wounded by someone to approach that person alone. Sometimes the sin is too deep, the abuse so severe and painful that victims should not approach their abuser alone. Appropriate pastoral care recognizes the need for nuance in each unique context, and pastors should not blanket-quote Matthew 6:15 ("But if you don't forgive others, neither will your Father forgive your sins") as if nuance and context are not important. A one-size-fits-all approach to pastoral care is almost never appropriate. Yes, forgiveness is an invitation for all, but we must exercise sensitivity and discernment toward those who are still healing from wounds done to them by another.[1]

---

1. Diane Leclerc and I explore more fully this important topic of paying attention to what we call the "sinned against" in our book, *The Back Side of the Cross: An Atonement Theology for the Abused and Abandoned* (Eugene, OR: Cascade Books, 2022).

brother or sister sins against you" (v. 15). People can sin un-intentionally. While teaching a class one time, I referenced a particular student in a joking manner. I did not mean to hurt that student with my joke, but I did. The relationship was damaged. Thankfully, with the help of another student, I was able to learn of the hurt I caused and apologize, re-pairing the relationship. It can be dangerous to assume that we have not sinned just because we did not intend to.

Jesus Lesson on Conflict #2: Take a Friend

But if they won't listen, take with you one or two others
so that every word may be established by the mouth of
two or three witnesses. (Matthew 18:16)

If we are in a situation where it is safe and appropriate to approach our offending brother or sister directly, Jesus has further instruction for what to do if this first step does not bring resolution: involve witnesses. Adding people to the conflict is not a tactic for ganging up on somebody; it is intended to help both parties find a way to reconcile. Ide-ally the witness will be a person (or persons) with healthy relationships on both sides of the conflict so that nobody feels cornered or attacked. Choosing this arbiter should be a matter of prayer. If this does not work, Jesus offers the next step.

Jesus Lesson on Conflict #3: Tell the Church

But if they still won't pay attention, report it to the church.
If they won't pay attention even to the church, treat them as
you would a Gentile and tax collector. (Matthew 18:17)

In Galatians 2, Paul appears to be relating the events of this step from his conflict with Peter. Scripture is not clear whether Paul tried steps 1 and 2 first, but it seems that the church hearing the complaint resolved this issue in regard to future practice.

When Jesus told them to treat them like gentiles or tax collectors, he was not encouraging condemnation or labeling them sinners or excluded by God. Remember in Matthew 8 Jesus said about a centurion—not simply a gentile, but a Roman soldier—who trusted Jesus to heal, "I say to you with all seriousness that even in Israel I haven't found faith like this" (v. 10). And in Matthew 21, Jesus announced to the chief priests and elders after sharing the parable of the two sons, "I assure you that tax collectors and prostitutes are entering God's kingdom ahead of you" (v. 31). So treating someone as a gentile or tax collector was to place that person outside the covenant community for a time, but it was important to continue to love and care for that person with the ultimate hope of eventual restoration.

Restoring Those Who Fall

Someone who has lost their way from the community is not to be cast off forever. The church must continue to reach out in the hope of welcoming them back into the body. James 5 encourages the church to never settle for a sister or brother who has wandered away (see vv. 19–20). Like Jesus leaving the ninety-nine to search for the one lost sheep, the church must always seek and welcome back those who have lost their way, treating them with a spirit of humble gentleness: "Brothers and sisters, if a person is caught doing something wrong, you who are spiritual should restore someone like this with a spirit of gentleness. Watch out for yourselves so you won't be tempted too" (Galatians 6:1). Perhaps one of the temptations Paul is talking about here is the temptation to approach a sinning person with condescending arrogance. Another temptation is believing that we ourselves would never fall away. Treat that sister or brother the same way you would want to be treated if you were to fall.

Christians Who Disagree

Of course, offending someone or saying something they don't want to hear is not *always* sinful. Context matters, and disagreement can occur between Christians without sin. Let's consider Jesus. Hebrews 4:15 testifies that Jesus did not sin. However, Jesus *did* offend people, and most of the time it was the pastors and theology professors from his own religious context. Offending someone because they don't want to receive a difficult truth is different from wounding someone because you were careless with your message. Jesus's instructions for conflict in Matthew 18 are for those who have sinned against one another, but they can also serve to guide us in cases of disagreements that lead to ruptured relationships or sin.

John Wesley's sermon "The Catholic Spirit" is also a helpful guide for Christians working through conflict. In that sermon, Wesley affirms this powerful hope: Even though we may not think alike may we love alike. May we be of one heart, though we are not of one opinion.[2] Wesley calls for humble charity among believers in areas of disagreement. Yet this charity does not mean we can't strongly express our opinions even as we do so humbly in love.

Unfortunately, some Christians have topics that are non-starters—which is to say they are so convinced of a particular viewpoint that they are unwilling to make space for dialogue. Since we do not live in a simple world, there are several hot-button issues where not all Christians agree—for example, abortion, LGBTQ+ rights, ordaining women, the death penalty, and racism, just to name a few. Trying to have charitable, loving, humble conversations on these issues is difficult because both sides earnestly

---

2. John Wesley, "Sermon 39: The Catholic Spirit," *Sermons I*, ed. Albert C. Outler, *The Bicentennial Edition of the Works of John Wesley*, vol. 2 (Nashville: Abingdon Press, 1976), paragraph 4.

believe their position is driven by their deep love for Jesus. Typically, these disagreements do not end well, and both parties walk away believing in their own rightness and the other person's sinfulness. It is important for us to be careful not to assume that our own opinions are always the most Christian. Let us learn from the mistakes of the self-righteous Pharisees.

Sowing Division

Having crucial, if difficult, conversations is beneficial, but sowing seeds of division is toxic. Paul's letters to Titus and the Romans offer many helpful instructions. In Titus he says, "Avoid stupid controversies, genealogies, and fights about the Law, because they are useless and worthless. After a first and second warning, have nothing more to do with a person who causes conflict, because you know that someone like this is twisted and sinful—so they condemn themselves" (3:9–11). In Romans Paul says, "Brothers and sisters, I urge you to watch out for people who create divisions and problems against the teaching that you learned. Keep away from them" (16:17).

Paul wanted the community to discern when conflict was necessary to work through and when people were sowing chaos for the sake of it. As a youth pastor and professor, I have always enjoyed robust conversation with my students. Through the years I have learned to discern when students were honestly seeking answers and when they were simply trying to create chaos. In the twenty-first century, social media has become an easy way to drop controversy bombs, baiting people into argument and conflict. Within the importance of good and hard conversations, Paul also warned about avoiding controversies with no life-bearing resolution. Such persons and practices should be removed like a cancer from the body. Every context needs thoughtful and prayerful discernment, but be wary of those who seem to be gifted at causing drama. They are likely acting in this way to offset pain in their own life that they are unwilling to deal with.

The pastor and church must not ignore or totally avoid conflict but learn to create mechanisms for *crucial conversations* that can address it. Creating an atmosphere of healthy conflict resolution cannot happen accidentally. The Holy Spirit's power to heal in and through good theological preaching and discussion is a beginning. Book studies that draw upon professionals in conflict resolution can also be helpful. One recommendation is the book *Crucial Conversations* along with the corresponding training.[3] A local church's inability to deal with conflict in healthy ways can become the primary evangelistic message that will invite others to run away. The way of empire squashes or eliminates conflict through violent coercion, but in the martyr church, patient listening and love guide resolution. A congregation known for its love in the face of conflict will be like a warm fire on a cold night to persons in the world looking for meaningful relationships that can last through life's storms.

---

3. Kerry Patterson, Joseph Grenny, and Ron McMillan, *Crucial Conversation: Tools for Talking When Stakes Are High* (New York, McGraw-Hill, 2012).

ELEVEN

To Those Who Have Been Hurt by the Church

What about those who were so deeply hurt by the church that they left? This chapter was not fun to write, but it is necessary. This chapter also requires a great deal of care and delicacy. I will not pretend this chapter is perfectly written or that it covers or says all that can or should be said. Above all, I do not want to sound simplistic or trite about an issue that has caused me deep grief concerning many who have left the church, and many more who have been hurt by the church.

Every person who has been hurt has a unique context and story. I have no desire to lump all persons into a generic narrative of pain. Wounds come from a variety of places, and although the global church—often in the form of local congregations but not always—has inflicted hurt across a broad spectrum throughout our long history, I want to address the general topics of trauma and abuse.

Specific kinds of teaching and preaching have caused trauma toward individuals who feel targeted, unwelcome, and devalued. Many people have reported psychological harm from the messages and practices that were part of their church experience, inflicting them with layers of toxic guilt and shame. Those preaching and teaching these messages likely felt they were doing what was right—yet great harm still occurred.

Other kinds of abuse and trauma have occurred not through Sunday school lessons, sermons, or weeknight Bible studies but through personal encounters. Whether the abusers are pastors or priests, Sunday school teachers, youth workers, volunteers, or just other laity in the church, trauma has been visited very particularly upon specific individuals.

I know people who have experienced both types of abuse and trauma from those in the church. For those whose trauma has been a result of sexism, racism, classism, and other -isms, the pain was likely caused in a variety of ways—through teaching and preaching, both implicitly and explicitly, and also through personal encounters with individuals, whether intentionally or otherwise. May God have mercy.

Many who have left the church will likely never read this. Of course it would be impossible to address every person and context properly here, but I pray that anyone who has been hurt by fellow Christians will have their pain named and acknowledged in the light as horrible, devastating, and evil. I also hope that if anyone who has left the church because of pain, trauma, or abuse does find their way into this chapter, these words will be heard and received in love. I want people to know that their hurt and pain has been ignored or silenced for far too long. We must bring to light and name the deeds that have been done in darkness.

This chapter is not simply a generic writing to a mass of nameless people. This chapter is hard and painful because I write to the names and faces that are carved into my very bones—family, friends, students, people I love deeply. To you specifically and to all I do not know, I offer these reflections. This is my intercessory lament.

To those who have been
Hurt by the church
Abused by the church
Silenced by the church
Guilted by the church
Rejected by the church

Ignored by the church
Shamed by the church
Dismissed by the church
To those who have been hurt by the church:

I

Am

Sorry

I confess and repent on behalf of the church.
We pastors have failed you.
I confess and repent that we have made your life worse,
not better.
We have offered you evil instead of grace.
There is no excuse.
Too often we have sought God's forgiveness but not yours.
We are wrong.
We are sorry.

As a pastor and theologian, I fully recognize that pain
will not evaporate as a result of reading this brief confession. For those who have suffered trauma or pain of any
kind, I hope and pray that you have sought or will seek
out professionals who, along with the Holy Spirit, can be
a means of grace and healing for you. While everyone's
abuse and trauma is unique, so too is everyone's path toward healing. I am hopeful that the church can help bring
to light what has too often been swept under the carpet,
kept in the dark, or spiritualized into oblivion. My colleague Diane Leclerc and I have written a book specifically

about atonement theology for those who have been sinned against called *The Back Side of the Cross*. Three brief points our book covers include the following.

First, forgiveness is not erasing the past as if it never happened. Forgiveness is about setting persons free from the captivity of past pain.

Second, while reconciliation may be possible, in some cases future healing and flourishing will mean relationships cannot return to what they were before. Some relationships will and should be ended, even in light of God's healing work.

Third, the victims of abuse always get to set the parameters for *how* and *when* forgiveness can be extended (see the accompanying WEC for elaboration).

Becoming and Being the Body of Christ

What follows in no way mitigates, dismisses, excuses, or normalizes any abuse or pain inflicted in the church. It should not ever happen. All the hurt and trauma that *have* happened simply demonstrate one aspect of the church as the body of the crucified and resurrected Christ that is *not yet* what the bride of Christ will and needs to become.

Yet we must be clear. Just as victims have names and faces, to say "the church" has caused pain and trauma is not to put the blame on some non-corporeal institution. The church is simply *people*. The church is people like me, who have gloriously failed at times to properly embody the love of God or failed to protect persons from abuse and trauma. The church—we as the body of Christ—each week confess and repent the ways we have hurt others and fallen short. These prayers are not simply empty rituals but practices that name the reality that there is more work and transformation yet to happen.

The church is a hospital, not a museum. And, as we know, *hurt people, hurt people*. This acknowledgment is not an excuse but a sad reality. Some may suggest this assertion

Wesleyan Ecclesial Confession

Too often Matthew 6:15 has been weaponized by the powerful to force forgiveness in a way that principally benefits only those who have done the wounding. Prevenient grace affirms that God is always working in our lives even when we don't know it or before we are ready to receive God's grace. As that has to do with forgiveness, God may work on someone's heart for many long years before they can even begin to think about forgiving the person who hurt them. It is not up to church leaders or any other Christians to make judgments or decisions about any individual's personal journey toward healing, forgiveness, and restoration. Although true forgiveness is the ultimate goal, the victim must be empowered to shape the process with the guidance of the Holy Spirit.

alone is reason enough to stay away. Certainly, some local churches are more toxic than others and should be closed. However, the vast majority of people in the church are working hard to be better at being loved and at loving others.

While *this is not an excuse,* when we think of the church as a hospital intended to help people heal instead of a museum of self-congratulatory admiration, we should not be surprised when people say or do things that are hurtful to others. I know of no place on earth that is entirely free of people hurting other people. Crime statistics show that persons are more likely to be harmed by people they know. The deeper the relationships, the greater the possibility for hurt and pain. Part of the intensity of the pain inflicted by the church comes as a result of the expectation that the church community *should* be a safe place in a violent and hostile world. When this expectation of safety goes unmet, the pain and abuse feel even more traumatic. It is not improper to expect the church to be a safe place, yet we must acknowledge that it does fail too often in our broken world.

Some may say, "Then why go? Why risk it?" Still more who have experienced pain and abuse ask, "Why stay?" These questions are valid and deserve to be considered individually on a case-by-case basis. Generally, if the issues have been a result of teaching and preaching, finding a new local church instead of giving up church altogether may be worthwhile. On the other hand, it is important to understand that those who have been abused and traumatized by church people may not have the courage or emotional energy to keep trying.

There may be a season when not participating in a local church can offer a time for healing and recovery. My prayerful hope is that this would be a season and not a permanent practice. While there are toxic expressions of Christianity that should not be accepted anywhere, most local churches are filled with people who are trying their best to be loved by God and then love others. This love happens amid ongoing bias, prejudice, ignorance, and our own lingering pain. The hope for the new creation God is bringing every day is that people, by the power of the Holy Spirit, can find a way to journey together despite the challenges that come with being in relationship. Moreover, the local church is likely to be one of the only places that can facilitate enduring relationships between people who thoroughly disagree. Most sectors of our life where we spend our free time are among people who look, act, and think like we do. Of course, there are exceptions, but the local church should be the perfect place for you and me to be challenged by each other to consider alternative perspectives for seeing the world. Disagreements and alternative perspectives are only beneficial in proportion to the level of intimacy and vulnerability we offer one another, which is a rare and special gift.

I do become a bit concerned when I hear things like, "I feel so much happier and more at peace since I left the church." When someone is leaving abuse and trauma, I fully understand. Yet if staying out of church becomes a permanent life habit for someone who claims to love and follow Jesus, I wonder how often they will engage voices and persons who may challenge their way of seeing the world. While it is fully understandable for wounded people to hesitate to expose themselves to further trauma, I do believe everyone can find a local church where they can be blessed while they bless others. God is uniquely at work in the world and in each of us, and God wants to be part of a person's ongoing flourishing life of love. Even if someone chooses not to gather formally in sanctuaries or cathedrals, I hope they can develop a meaningful community of committed relationships with Christians who can be a central part of their life.

To victims, let me again say I am so sorry for the pain and trauma you have suffered. God weeps with you; I weep with you. What happened should not have happened. I pray that, despite the pain, God will lead you into the waters of healing and hope, where what was done to you does not define you. Know that God loves you and that many faithful Christians will seek to love you too as you find the courage to be vulnerable again.

To Church Leaders

Friends, I love the church, and I love my brothers and sisters in the faith, but we must do better. There are many reasons why people choose not to participate in local communities of faith, but one area where the church can confess its shortcoming and commit to ongoing maturity is lamentation.

First, we must provide more space in all our rhythms of liturgical activity to allow people to express lament. A friend of mine offered a devastating update on social media about being excited to move forward with a fresh start and gain distance from the tragedies he and his family had experienced over the course of the previous year. Not too long after that hope-filled post, my friend became ill and was diagnosed with leukemia. He wrote another post describing simply and honestly his raw pain and heartache. He shared a picture of himself in his hospital gown heading into a chemo treatment with his wife by his side. With tears running down their faces, the picture featured both of them holding up their middle fingers in a heartbreaking symbol of their anger, pain, and grief. This couple was determined to fight, but they were also angry and afraid. This couple needed a local congregation who could in solidarity raise a middle finger with them against cancer—but also against God. Even in their pain and anger, they were not pushing God away but, like Job, angrily demanding that God be present to their pain and protest. If the church cannot create space in communal worship for giving God the middle finger in pain and protest, the raising of hands in praise feels empty and dishonest.

Some local churches offer Blue Christmas services during the Advent season. While Advent and Christmas are seasons of joy for many, they are also extremely painful for those who have experienced loss, tragedy, and hardship. These services create intentional space in the middle of a season that becomes especially difficult for those who are hurting to offer their cries of pain, hurt, and despair. People who are in pain need a place to express their sorrow and anger in a community of faith that can stand with them and mourn with them (see Romans 12:15).

Not only do we offer laments for those who are facing life's hardships, but the church must also cry out and name what has been done inside and outside the church fellowship. We must no longer dismiss, hide, or silence people and their pain. Guided by professional counselors, churches can offer healthy means of sharing pain and abuse where the church can come alongside and journey with people in their pain. Wesleyans who believe in the gift of entire sanctification must confess the sins that have been done to us and the sins that have been done against others. Too often, rather than listening with compassion, our insecurity and defensiveness shoot the wounded and, in the worst cases, blame victims for what was done to them. Lord, have mercy!

Second, background checks, both formal and informal, should be done for every type of leadership position in the church. Some of the most persistent toxic behavior by leaders in the church will not show up on a formal background check. References from previous assignments and local churches should be consulted with great intentionality. This action is not an attempt to create prejudice, perpetuate unfair ostracism, or encourage gossip, but too often bad behavior among Christian leaders goes unaddressed. Rather than be confronted and challenged to confess and repent, unhealthy Christian leaders are too often allowed to move on to the next assignment where they will be free to continue exercising their unhealthy leadership models and practices with new, vulnerable people. Of course, this reality can apply to lay members as well. In all parts of church leadership structures, we need to be more intentional about protecting people of all ages from those who have hurt others in the past.

Third, we must confess the teaching and preaching that have caused devastating trauma. In small groups, in Sunday school classes, in home groups, in prayer meetings, and beyond, we must not silence those who need to share about the ways they have been hurt by the church. As a pastor I can look back on my ministry of more than thirty years and name more than one occasion when I ignorantly offered something other than the true gospel of Christ. The gospel of Jesus Christ never needs to use fear or guilt as a manipulative tool. Friends, we do not need to be defensive in response to people's stories of pain. We must listen, apologize, and seek to do better. While there is a need to discern whining from lamenting, it is important to create a safe atmosphere where people can talk through the joys and also the pains of life.

Fourth, *love, love, love*. Our posture must remain loving. We can be sad and disappointed about those who have left, but our love must remain constant.

Much, much more can be said. This chapter is hard and not fun. At its core, the martyr church works to be present with persons in their anger and despair. We need the triune God's help to be a better hospital—not a hospital where no one finds healing but a hospital that leans into the One who, as Henri Nouwen noted, is the *wounded Healer*. The kingdom of God in this new creation is for all.

Let us participate in what God is doing to make it so. As one beggar finds bread, may we help all sisters and brothers find both daily bread and the Bread of Life. May we never become obstacles to God's healing and grace.

The Political Mission of the Church

Now we'll explore how the martyr church participates in the coming of God's new creation kingdom as its political mission in the world. Jesus did not come to earth to provide a way for humans to leave. The martyr church does not condemn the earth or seek escape from it. Conversely, the martyr church seeks to participate in Christ, who immersed God in creation in order that the new creation can come more fully to earth as it is in heaven. The church— the body of the crucified and resurrected Christ—is invited by the power of the Spirit to participate in God's ongoing bringing of the new creation kingdom. This new creation is here in part but will yet come in fullness to the glory of God.

The mission of the martyr church is part of a liturgical breathing of the local and global church. The Holy Spirit gathers (breathes in) the local church in communal worship. In this communion, the local church is healed and renewed as the body of Christ through a divine-human encounter. This encounter is part of an ongoing transformation. Yet the final goal of the communion of local worship does not end when the pastor says the benediction. The benediction is a blessing *with* a commission

159

to go out and participate in God's ministry, working toward the renewal and redemption of all things. In this way, communal worship breathes in the local body to be then *blown out* by and with the Spirit to participate in God's mission in the world.

Communion moves to mission. If communion does not lead to mission, it becomes toxic and stagnant. Yet what is the goal and purpose of mission? Communion. Too often, well-meaning believers who get frustrated with communal worship attempt to engage in mission that is disconnected from the local church. Yet if mission does not invite persons who are lost and marginalized into the discipleship of communion, then mission can be reduced to charity. For example, feeding the poor and clothing the naked is not enough. Those things are important, but the full hope is to enter into relationships of *kindred mutuality* with those we encounter in mission, bringing them into the communion of the local church. We are breathed in for communion to be breathed out for mission to then be breathed back in for communion, and on and on.[1]

---

1. See my book *Created to Worship*, available from The Foundry Publishing, where I explore this rhythm more fully, especially on pages 41–45.

TWELVE

Rejecting Dualism and Empire

As I grew up in U.S. Christian culture, I began to notice the Christians around me using labels that created an intense dualism. Things were either Christian (and therefore sacred), or pagan, heathen, or worldly (and therefore secular). The biggest one was, of course, Christian music versus pagan music. There were lists created of bands where one column listed a secular band, and across from it in the second column was the name of a Christian band that was supposed to be similar in style and sound. This comparison tactic was meant to get teens listening to Christian bands instead of heathen music, but the music world was not the only arena where this label game was played. There were also Christian movies and secular movies, Christian businesses and worldly businesses, Christian spaces and secular spaces. Everything was categorized as one or the other—even the two major U.S. political parties. By the time I was in high school, I found the labels to be tired and unhelpful, but it was not until grad school that I was given the language of "sacred-secular dualism."

Christians in the U.S. created this dualism in order to mark clear boundaries in the world of what was Christian and holy and what was definitely not. These boundaries marked who was in and who was out, leading to a culture of harsh judgment and a spirit of condemnation toward those things and people that Christians considered "worldly." Labeling everything as one of two things in a good-versus-evil binary resulted in Christians urging one another not to engage with anything that fell on the secular side, lest we become defiled by the unholy. The practice became so widespread that the church still struggles today with the temptation toward the sacred-secular dualism. Rather than fulfilling the Great Commission by loving and proclaiming God's forgiveness of sin and making disciples, a large portion of Christians from that cultural era chose separation from the world, creating an entire subculture of Christian self-righteousness, judgmentalism, and elitism that are antithetical to the gospel of Christ. Secular-sacred dualism is not a Christlike way to approach the world.

Dualism that affirms places and people where God is and other places and people where God is not, is *false*. God is present in all the world, even in the places where evil is thick, powerful, and toxic. Such dualism also imagines that God favors and loves some more than others, and of course we always imagine ourselves to be in the group God loves. When Christians affirm that some people are less loved by God, then Christians feel justified committing atrocious acts against them—or, if not committing those acts ourselves, at least permitting others to commit them. Racism and sexism—and all the other sinful -isms that have been problems within the church as well as out in the world— are laid on the foundation of othering and dehumanization that begins with dualism.

Although a strictly enforced dualism is not the way of Christ, it is also important to recognize that almost nothing in life can be considered neutral. Some forms of culture, art, entertainment, hobbies, activities, and relationships will be more life-giving than others. As the apostle Paul affirms in 1 Corinthians 6:12, "I have the freedom to do anything, but not everything is helpful. I have the freedom to do anything, but I won't be controlled by anything." I do come from the Holiness tradition within Christendom, which seeks continually to be healed in God's holiness in order to love more deeply. There is a great danger for persons who claim to be Christians when their lives could not be distinguished from those whose lives are patterned around practices glorifying death, exploitation, and objectification. Christians are to be a distinct, unique, peculiar people being transformed into the image of the crucified and resurrected Christ.

There are two specific points to make about rejecting the sacred-secular dualism.

First, the posture of the kingdom of God and the church toward the world is not one of condescending judgment, fearful hostility, or pious elitism. The posture of Jesus Christ and the kingdom he inaugurated seeks to transform, heal, redeem, and renew all things. This is the goal and hope of the new creation kingdom. Our posture is always to be one of humble love and servanthood.

Second, when we reject sacred-secular dualism, that does not mean we advocate a version of relative truth where everything is declared neutral, neither positive nor negative. Conversely, every piece of art, media, and practice continually shapes our lives for better or worse. What we do really does matter. How we spend our time, money, and what we consume are all things that continually shape us. The question remains: what things in our lives help us conform more into the image of Jesus, and what things pull us away from that image toward death and nothingness? Do we smell of the fragrance of Christ or the odor of death?

The Seduction of Empire as Nationalism

One of the great challenges for the church in the United States in the twenty-first century is battling the temptation of empire to merge (or *syncretize*) Christianity with nationalism, which seduces us into replacing God as our source of hope, security, and peace. This temptation has history going all the way back to ancient Israel. The Old Testament teaches us about what happened when the Israelites were seduced by empire into wanting a king like all the other nations had. In 1 Samuel 1, God heard Hannah's cry and blessed her with a child, Samuel, whom she gave to the Lord. Hannah gave Samuel to Eli the priest to be raised in the house of the Lord (see 1 Samuel 1:24–28). The Lord rejected Eli's wicked sons for the role of prophet and instead called out to young Samuel (see 1 Samuel 3).

Samuel served the Lord faithfully as a prophet for God's people in what was intended to be the Israelites' political system. God was their supreme authority, and God would use prophets to help guide and lead the people into more fully becoming God's distinctive people in order to be a source of hope, blessing, and joy for *all* peoples of the earth. This unique political system was about keeping Yahweh as the center of hope, life, joy, protection, and future. Another feature of those who desired to be faithful to Yahweh's covenant was the invitation to never be settled in the land. From the moment the Israelites were delivered from Egypt, they were led physically by Yahweh. This physical leading symbolically connected to Yahweh's religious and political leadership.

In her helpful book *Church on the Way*, Nell Becker Sweeden notes the essential character and gift of the church never becoming too comfortable and secure in a particular location. "There is something important about the church's identity remaining on the margins and characterized by diaspora that preserves distance from the world's status quo."[1] The nomadic sojourn following the exodus from Egypt was more than geographical; it should have liturgically shaped

1. Nell Becker Sweeden, *Church on the Way: Hospitality and Migration* (Eugene, OR: Pickwick Publications, 2015), Kindle version.

Wesleyan Ecclesial Confession

The church needs to live into an imagination of sojourning. When we become too settled, we risk falling into idolatrous practices that tempt us to love creation more than the Creator and distract us from keeping God as our primary hope and imagination.

this distinct people of God. When we return to the prophet Samuel, who had a long and faithful ministry, 1 Samuel describes the Israelites' growing envy as they noticed the one commonality all the nations around them shared: they all had kings. Like Eli's sons before Samuel, Samuel's own sons were not obedient to God (8:3). The Israelites used the shortcomings of Samuel's sons to argue that they should have a king because Samuel had no fit successor. The Lord saw right through their duplicity. Just as God found and empowered Samuel, even though Eli's sons were disobedient, God could have raised up another faithful prophet outside of Samuel's family.

Samuel was not happy with the people's request for a king, and he brought his concern to the Lord.

> The LORD answered Samuel, "Comply with the people's request—everything they ask of you—because they haven't rejected you. No, they've rejected me as king over them. They are doing to you only what they've been doing to me from the day I brought them out of Egypt to this very minute, abandoning me and worshipping other gods. So comply with their request, but give them a clear warning, telling them how the king will rule over them."
> (1 Samuel 8:7–9)

The Israelites were not rejecting Samuel, nor were they actually concerned about Samuel's unqualified sons; instead, they were rejecting the Lord. The Lord's word to Samuel is painful because it confirms that the request for a king fell in line with centuries of Israelite disobedience. Although the Lord had gotten the Israelites out of Egypt, the Israelites had not gotten the Egyptian habits and empire imagination out of themselves.

The Lord told Samuel to announce to the Israelites what a king would be like—all the ways a king would use and abuse them, oppress them, and tax them (see 1 Samuel 8:10–17). Samuel ended with a warning: "When that day comes, you will cry out because of the king you chose for yourselves, but on that day the LORD won't answer you" (v. 18). This warning should be filed under *be careful what you wish for*. But the people were politically committed to rejecting Yahweh as their King, and they refused to listen to Samuel's warnings (see vv. 19–20). What the Israelites failed to realize was that they had started down the slippery slope of yielding to the seductions of empire. The church must never look to itself or to any other political authority for safety, hope, and protection. The church must continue to let God fight for us as our source of protection and hope.

After the people refused to listen, the Lord told Samuel to go ahead and give them what they asked for (v. 22). One could argue that this level of religious disobedience—desiring a human to be king and not Yahweh—was one of the most tragic acts of disobedience in all of Scripture. All those things the Lord warned that a king would to do them, their kings did. In Deuteronomy 17 there is also a list of things a king must not do. The king should not acquire too many horses, return to Egypt to get more horses, have too many wives, or acquire too much gold or silver (Deuteronomy 17:16–17). Sadly, 1 Kings recounts that Solomon did all those things (see 1 Kings 9–10).[2] Even as the wisest of all the kings, Solomon still embodied the religious and political syncretism (the merging of multiple beliefs and allegiances) that cast a shadow on all the future monarchs of the divided kingdoms. This narrative is a cautionary tale for the church today: we must never make the mistake of thinking we can have equal allegiance to a country and to God.

---

2. Thanks to T. Scott Daniels for pointing these two references out to me.

The Rise of Nationalism

"Normal" is often defined by what is familiar, and what is familiar shapes the lens for how we see the world. Only after meaningful encounters with other people who have different lenses can we begin to see our own lives more objectively. Diversity is a marvelous gift of God's creation. We may be threatened by differences if we are enslaved by insecurity, but when we choose courage and curiosity over fear, we become able to appreciate and celebrate others' distinctiveness, which can in turn help us see our own lens (and bias) more clearly. For example, I never realized how much it rained and how little sun there was in Seattle, Washington—until I moved to Phoenix, Arizona.

My life growing up was homogenous, white, middle class, and churched. I had a wonderful life, but it was comfortable and sheltered, which inhibited my ability to understand that my normal wasn't everybody's normal. On the other hand, my safe and comfortable foundation gave me confidence in myself to be open to learning from others. Because I felt secure in my own context and background, I did not feel threatened when I began to encounter those who had different contexts and backgrounds from my own. I have been blessed through the years to be able to travel around the globe and meet amazing people from diverse cultures. Only as I began to travel to different places and meet new people did I begin to more clearly see myself and world I had grown up in.

Because I grew up in the 1980s, one of my favorite movies was *Rocky IV*. For those who have not yet been blessed with this exquisite cinematic experience, this movie takes place mostly in "the evil empire" of Russia as Rocky Balboa fights Ivan Drago. Previously, Ivan killed Apollo Creed in what was to be an exhibition match in the U.S. So Rocky goes to Russia to train, away from all the comforts of the U.S., which have made him soft. Rocky is not only fighting Ivan Drago but also all of Mother Russia. Rocky trains with limited barn equipment—carts and bales of hay—in a remote region where he has to run up and down mountains and cannot rely on any of the comforts from home he has grown used to. Rocky's training in Russia is contrasted with Drago, who is making use of advanced technology, a team of trainers, and performance-enhancing drugs. This movie reflected my view of Russia: Russia was like the U.S. in many ways, but there was one key difference: Russia was "evil" while the U.S. was "good." When I look back now, it is plain to see how this film lived into the stereotypical U.S. propaganda of the Cold War era.

During my senior year of high school in 1993, I had the privilege of traveling to Moscow as part of a small singing tour group from my Christian high school. I was not prepared for what I encountered. In 1991, Boris Yeltsin was the first elected president of Russia. There was a great deal of chaos and corruption following the breakup of the USSR, and we arrived directly in the middle of this climate. Russia was not an "evil" version of the USA. We found it to be bleak and colorless; a general sense of depression weighed heavily everywhere we went. It was clear these people were not our enemy. They were hungry, tired, and often in despair. This was my first real experience where I began to see how "American" I really was. (And, of course, I now recognize that even the term "American" itself is not monocultural, since it encompasses two entire continents all the way from the southern tip of Chile to the northern edge of Canada.) God helped move me to compassion from a place of competitive fear. My lens was being adjusted.

We were able to sing our Christian concert in public schools, town halls, and orphanages. One of the schools we visited was full of children whose parents had died in the Chernobyl disaster of 1986. It was humbling—and now feels a bit condescending—to sing about Christian hope to these people who had suffered so deeply.

We also traveled to a small village in Ukraine, where we approached what we were told was a church. On the outside, it was an ordinary, plain, non-descript building. When we went inside, we were absolutely blown away. It was one of the most beautiful sanctuaries I had ever seen, with exquisite carvings and woodwork that were on par with the vast cathedrals across Europe for their beauty and ability to evoke the holy in sacred space. We met the pastor and several church members. During our tour of the sanctuary, they showed us a place where they would hide the children when the soldiers came. During the height of the USSR, it was illegal to be Christian. The pastor and members shared stories about many in the church who had been shot outside the sanctuary for their faith. The pastor said there was a time when to be gathered in that space for worship meant a willingness to die. A thought hit me for the first time that I have never been able to shake: *Would I be willing to go to communal worship if it meant I might die that day?* As a high school senior, I was not sure of my answer. This Ukrainian congregation was a faithful expression of the martyr church—not seeking death but not fearing it.

Nationalism tempts the church away from God's kingdom and toward the kingdom of empire. One of the dangers for the church that has existed for quite some time is to naively merge our Christian faith with loyalty to our country. There have been seasons in my life when I was more United States American than Christian. I love this country and feel blessed to have been born in it, but I can now see how my reliance on the United States has at times been more powerful than my trust in God. The United States, like many other nations today and throughout history, embodies a form of empire that can lure Christians into putting our hope and trust in something other than God.

The Seduction of Empire

Scott Daniels has written a helpful book exploring the letters written to the churches in Revelation. Although there are many essential themes to examine, the seduction of empire is a core theme that demands the church's vigilance. Revelation, more than predicting or revealing the end times, is first and foremost a revelation of Jesus Christ as the Lamb of God who was slain and who is the victory of all. This revelation of Christ is juxtaposed with cautions for God's people who may be seduced away from the kingdom of God and the martyr church.

The letter to Pergamum warns about the danger of accommodation (2:12–17). Pergamum was not a center of economic power or commercial success, but it was a key religious and political city. Revelation is clear in the assertion that all religions are political, and all politics are religious. Daniels notes that, because of its economic limitations, Pergamum would find its joy and purpose by "orienting the city toward bringing glory to the empire."[3] Although Pergamum could never equal the glory and splendor of Rome, it would try to be a perfect reflection, or image, of Rome.[4] When people visited Pergamum, the hope was "that they would know there is a powerful empire in the world because the empire's life would be reflected in the life of the city."[5] Hence, one of the means to achieve this goal was through the emperor worship. Rome rewarded Pergamum for its empire loyalty by giving it the authority to be the judgment seat of Rome in the east. Additionally, Pergamum hosted violent gladiatorial games as a liturgical practice of embodying and glorifying the power of Rome.

---

3. T. Scott Daniels, *Seven Deadly Spirits: The Message of Revelation's Letters for Today's Church* (Grand Rapids: Baker Academic, 2009), 64.

4. Daniels, *Seven Deadly Spirits*, 64.

5. Daniels, *Seven Deadly Spirits*, 64.

Daniels notes that, of the seven cities addressed in Revelation, the church in Pergamum was the one likely to clash with the powerful emperor worship.[6] How would the church bear witness to and glorify Christ in a city whose identity and source of power was its glorification of the emperor and Rome? Would they respond to the invitation of the martyr church or be seduced by the promises of empire? The reference in Revelation 2:14 to Balaam's teaching likely means that some within the church "were teaching that accommodation with the culture was the wisest political party. . . . The sin of the church at Pergamum was spiritual laxity and tolerance without spiritual discernment."[7] This church appeared to maintain worship of Christ while also trying to fit in with the surrounding culture and, thus, was losing its way. However, not all in Pergamum had failed. The letter begins with an affirmation of those who were "holding onto my [God's] name" and a celebration of the faithful witness of Antipas, who appears to have been a martyr (2:13). In the Pergamum church, it appears that some were faithful while others wanted a faith that did not put them at odds with the civic cultural power of the day.

One of the keys to Rome's success was their *Pax Romana* policy, which essentially allowed persons to practice their own religion as long as they were also willing to pay homage to the Roman gods. This is not the way of Christianity! The triune God who loves and cares deeply for us is a jealous God who recognizes that allowing accommodation (or syncretism) is lethal.

What does it mean to have a faith that is happy to worship Jesus but also bows the knee to other cultural religions like materialism, consumerism, militarism, nationalism, and on and on?

---

6. Daniels, *Seven Deadly Spirits*, 65
7. Daniels, *Seven Deadly Spirits*, 66.

What does it mean when Christians today can more easily recite a nation's pledge of allegiance than a Christian creed?

How is the empire today seducing Christians in practices and behaviors that appear innocent and harmless but in the end are deeply toxic?

From Abraham forward into the body of Christ, the calling of God's people—Christ's church—is to be unique in order to become a blessing to all the world. While many have come to know and be part of the body of Christ, many others have attempted to have dual citizenship—allegiances to both church and empire. The church must resist the devastating temptations of empire. In light of the inbreaking kingdom of God, the church is not living in exile but is a foretaste of the new creation that is irrupting in the world.

Resident Aliens in the Kingdom of God

The church as the body of Christ walks in between two extremes. One extreme is the allure of empire, where the church is simply assimilated and believes the primary goal is trying to make the world nicer while living according to the rules and cultures of the world. The other extreme is the sacred-secular dualism, which celebrates a desire to leave this sinful earth and escape to heaven with strong insider-outsider imagination.

Between these two extremes, the church is invited to live as resident aliens in the world God created, celebrating that Christ's kingdom has *already* arrived while recognizing it is *not yet* fully realized. In his important book *Surprised by Hope*, N.T. Wright notes that the new creation is not somewhere else but is coming like a faithful ferment here and now. As with all notions of eschatology (thoughts on the end times), there is a great sense of *already* that was fully inaugurated through Jesus Christ and continues to come daily as God's kingdom comes to earth as in heaven. Yet there is a great hope of the *not-yet*.

Agreeing with Paul that Christians are resident aliens does not mean that our goal is to abandon the earth; instead, it means we recognize that the powers of empire are not permanent. Yet, if those powers and principalities are present, we in the church must live distinct from them. As resident aliens, we are not afraid of the world; we do not hate the world; we are not trying to escape the world—yet we resist allegiance to the empires of the world. We are sent by God in the power of the Spirit to love the world. We are invited to participate in God's work in the further inbreaking of this kingdom, as heaven more fully comes to earth.

So what might it look like for the church to love its neighbor? First, how well do we know our neighbors? What are the needs of the community? How can we partner with other organizations in our community seeking to provide compassionate mutuality amidst advocacy? How can the church better journey with those who are struggling to find affordable housing? How can the church better help advocate for those who need legal assistance or medical care? This is evangelism, this is compassion, this is discipleship. This is the church finding contextual ways to be a better neighbor to those in our communities, especially those with whom Jesus would be spending most of his time.

The church is sent into the world in hope and joy and, with Micah, to walk humbly, to love mercy, and to do justice (see Micah 6:8). We are a people of hope, love, and mercy who speak against injustice, advocate for the marginalized, and work to be present to those in pain and despair. This is our vocation, which is how we live into Christ's prayer in John 14, continuing the works that Christ began and allowing the Spirit to use us in all the places where the hope, life, forgiveness, and joy of the new creation have not yet dawned.

THIRTEEN

Hospitality in the Martyr Church

In light of the cautions about sacred-secular dualism, nationalism, and the allure of empire, how shall the church participate in God's mission in the world?

After God promised to be Israel's protector and help restore them as a people in Micah 5, the Lord told them in Micah 6 what was required of God's people: "He has told you, human one, what is good and what the LORD requires from you: to do justice, embrace faithful love, and walk humbly with your God" (v. 8). Sadly, Christians in the twenty-first century are not always in agreement about what it looks like to do justice, embrace faithful love, and walk humbly.

Jesus is the model and means, not only of the church's salvation but also for how the martyr church should participate in the further coming of the kingdom of God. Brian Zahnd points out that Martin "Luther referred to the risky way of Jesus that is marked by humility, obedience, and vulnerability standing in sharp contrast to and in opposition to the hunger for *empire glory*. The 'way of the cross,' for Luther, is demanding and costly because it contradicts the dominant way of the world."[1] It is always tempting to engage the church's mission using the methods of empire.

1. Brian Zahnd, *Postcards from Babylon: The Church in American Exile* (Spello Press, 2019), Kindle Edition, loc. 44.

Instead, the church must embrace love for enemies and resist the temptation to violence.

Loving Enemies

There are concepts, practices, and rituals in Christianity that do not feel strange to those who were raised in the church but would seem odd to outsiders. It was probably not until college that I actually considered it odd to imagine that God became a human and walked on this earth. From Moses parting the Red Sea to Elijah calling down fire from heaven to Jesus walking on water, my life was immersed in the stories of Scripture that I accepted without question. As I have grown and my faith has matured, I have had to wrestle with things I easily embraced as a child.

One of the hardest areas for many Christians—even children—to embrace is the call to love enemies. "Regardless of what Caesar might do with the sword of vengeance, and however we might envision God accomplishing sovereign purposes through a pagan government, followers of Jesus are called to renounce revenge and love their enemies. To follow Jesus's command to love enemies is clear we are not to kill them. Always. This is the Jesus way."[2] Jesus's command to love enemies means we do not kill them.

To more fully become the body and blood of Christ, the church is called to actively pursue justice and righteousness—but non-violently. "The Christian is countercultural not just in opposition to the powers that be—for opposition can easily adopt the violent means that both Jesus and Paul condemned—but in opposition to violent power altogether. The sword is never really countercultural, but the cross always is."[3] This call to love enemies and engage nonviolently in justice is the distinctive calling for the martyr church.

---

2. Zahnd, *Postcards from Babylon*, loc. 12–13.

3. Zahnd, *Postcards from Babylon*, loc. 16.

Church as a Journeying People

One of the insidious dangers of a deep-seeded blending of the church with nationalism is that nations have different goals and purposes than the church does. As the martyr church lives into the image of the crucified and resurrected Christ, the primary goal of the church is not to seek its own survival at all costs; the primary goal of the church is faithfulness. As disciples of Jesus Christ, we are not on a quest to build private kingdoms of wealth, prestige, safety, or permanence. Rather, the great joy of the martyr church is the invitation of Christ to find life by giving it away.

Eugene Peterson's translation of the Bible puts it this way: "Give away your life; you'll find life given back, but not merely given back—given back with bonus and blessing. Giving, not getting, is the way. Generosity begets generosity" (Luke 6:38, MSG). The way of the Christ is the way of the cross; this is the way to respond in thanksgiving and praise to the life, healing, and redemption of God—by giving our lives away, especially to the stranger. Revelation is clear that living as disciples of the martyr church who bear the image of the slaughtered Lamb, may mean our physical life is taken (see 6:9–11). The goal of the martyr is never to seek death, but that possibility exists. That possibility is why the church is a pilgrim people of *resident aliens* who refuse to live or act out of fear or with the primary goal of safety, security, and happiness while others starve at our gates.

Christians should not be comfortable and settled while anyone is hungry, homeless, or alone. To be the kingdom people of the martyr church is to see all persons as gifts from God, whom we are invited to love and be loved by. Having eyes to see and ears to hear is an essential posture that invites us to really *see* the other. Emmanuel Lévinas prophetically urges us to let the other's face hold us captive.[4] This seeing, this presence, opens us up to the new gifts of each person we encounter. In this way the primary ethic of the martyr church is to embody hospitality toward the world.

Nell Becker Sweeden says, "The people of God are sojourners, journeying toward the heavenly kingdom, yet also making God's reign visible on earth. Hospitality practice re-conceived as journey and accompaniment with those deemed 'other' directs ecclesial communities toward deeper faithfulness in their identity and mission in the world."[5]

In this subtle way the church refuses hard walls of exclusion. To see life as a sojourn of hospitality creates a new lens for seeing the world, where people are invited and welcomed into the journey. Becker Sweeden goes on: "Hospitality is a bodily manifestation of the church's identity and witness before the world. Rooted in baptism and the Eucharist, hospitality practice reminds the church of its identity and heritage as a pilgrim people and points it forward to go out, encounter others, and build relationships along the way."[6] The church as the body of Christ continues into a life of being present to welcome the stranger into this journey of the already-but-not-yet kingdom of new creation.

---

4. "[The face] captivates by its grace as by magic, but does not reveal itself. If the transcendent cuts across sensibility, if it is openness preeminently, if its vision is the vision of the very openness of being, it cuts across the vision of forms and can be stated neither in terms of contemplation nor in terms of practice. It is the face; its revelation is speech. The relation with the Other alone introduces a dimension of transcendence, and leads us to a relation totally different from experience in the sensible sense of the term, relative and egoist." Emmanuel Lévinas, *Totality and Infinity: An Essay on Exteriority* (Pittsburgh: Duquesne University Press, 1969), 193.

5. Becker Sweeden, *Church on the Way*, 147.

6. Becker Sweeden, *Church on the Way*, 147.

Seeking Justice for All: Allies and Advocacy

The Spirit empowers the martyr church to participate in God's work to redeem all things as the new creation comes more fully to earth. In this way, the church is called to continue the ministry of the incarnation. This ministry is certainly one of advocacy *for* and *with* those who have been pushed to the empire's margins. The empire's margins are the center of Christ's crucified and resurrected presence. Jesus spent most of his recorded ministry in the Gospels with those who were being exploited by both civic and religious authorities. What was it about Christ that those who felt shunned by the powers of the land (including religious leaders) pursued him? It certainly was not because he offered a message that did not challenge them. Jesus often invited persons to stop sinning and follow him. We must see our participation in caring for the naked, homeless, and orphan as uniting our mission with evangelism. We bear witness by sharing the love of Christ.

Finding God and the Church
in the Margins of Empire

Too often I have taught and preached about the church *going* to care for the poor, naked, and oppressed. This mindset is a failure that actually reinforces sacred-secular dualism. In the call to participate in God's mission of hospitality in the world by being present to "the least of these" (Matthew 25:40), a few things must be learned. Eric Severson offers a gripping engagement of the Matthew 25 text throughout church history in his book *The Least of These.* In Matthew 25, the king celebrates righteous sheep who feed the hungry, give water to the thirsty, show hospitality to the stranger, clothe the naked, take care of the sick, and visit those in prison. The king declares that when they have done these acts of kindness "for one of the least of these brothers and sisters of mine, you have done it for me" (v. 40). Conversely, when the goats failed to do any of these same activities, they have abandoned and failed to love God (v. 45).

The parable of the sheep and the goats illuminates my careless error. The church does not *go* to the poor but finds that God and the church are already present in and among the poor. John Wesley affirmed that in visiting the poor, the sick, those in prison, and individuals in despair, we see and encounter the face of God.[7] Severson powerfully affirms that the "church is an event that happens when the hungry are fed, the naked are clothed, widows are cared for, and prisoners are visited."[8] To state it more directly: when the poor, naked, hungry, widow, and orphan are not present in the communal gathering of believers, then God is not fully present, and the gathering is not really the church. Too often Christians have called "church" a gathering of the victors of empire. Too often these gatherings have been self-congratulatory for winning empire games, neglecting God by relegating the marginalized to patronized charity.

Often those who have not experienced injustice may have a hard time initially understanding the cries from those who experience injustice and oppression all the time. John Wesley confirms such difficulty:

> One great reason why the rich, in general, have so little sympathy for the poor is because they so seldom visit them. Hence it is that, according to the common observation, one part of the world does not know what the other suffers. Many of them do not know, because they do not care to know: they keep out of the way of

---

7. See Wesley, "Sermon 98, On Visiting the Sick," *Sermons III, Works of John Wesley* vol. 3.

8. This insight emerged through personal correspondence between Severson and myself.

Wesleyan Ecclesial Confession

In the martyr church, we cannot claim to love God if we have not cared for and been compassionate toward persons with physical, social, and emotional needs. The sanctifying love of God is seen primarily in how we love other humans—especially those on the margins of empire.

knowing it—and then plead their voluntary ignorances as an excuse for their hardness of heart.[9]

Those who have benefited from a strong allegiance to empire often silence those who are abused by empire. Sadly, this silence is demanded not only by those who explicitly cause the abuse but often also by many who simply want to keep the status quo.[10]

Martin Luther King, Jr., in his prophetic "Letter from Birmingham Jail," exhorts, "Injustice anywhere is a threat to justice everywhere. We are caught in an inescapable network of mutuality, tied in a single garment of destiny. Whatever affects one directly, affects all indirectly."[11] What King is talking about here is precisely the notion that all people are tied together as one body of humanity. Yet, as a white, middle-class man, I am also challenged from all the places of privilege and power from which I come. My silence speaks loudly to affirm the status quo and permit oppression. Again, Dr. King prophetically speaks right to my bones: "In the end we will not remember the words of our enemies but the silence of our friends."[12] For the martyr church, an important first step for those who have not experienced oppression and injustice is to listen and be present. Listen to those in pain. Listen to those who are exhausted and tired of the struggle and feel like no one cares. This listening then needs deep reflection and further education to let it soak into our marrow. The first step out of silence is listening.

There are two polarizing justice movements that have gripped the United States in recent years. These two movements have divided Christians because they have convicted

---

9. Wesley, "On Visiting the Sick," *Works of John Wesley*, 387–88.

10. See Walter Brueggemann's *Prophetic Imagination* (Minneapolis: Fortress Press, 2001).

11. Martin Luther King, Jr., "Letter from Birmingham Jail," April 16, 1963.

12. Martin Luther King, Jr., "Letter from Birmingham Jail," April 16, 1963.

us, made us feel uncomfortable, made us wonder how we may have been complicit in the collective acts of sin these movements have sought to highlight and protest. Justice movements are rarely executed with perfect flawlessness, but they are part of the kingdom of God coming more fully to earth.

#MeToo

Our canonized Scriptures emerged from and reflected the cultures from which they were birthed. As we have already discussed, the Scriptures offer clear evidence that patriarchy is a result of the disease of sin in our world. The historically poor treatment of women by men is certainly part of creation's groaning and crying out testified to in Romans 8:19–23. Sadly, there has never been a time in the history of the world when men were not dominating, controlling, or abusing women, even deep into the twenty-first century.

Hopefully a new day is dawning. More women are confronting and naming the abuse and exploitation that, for too long, have remained in the dark. Some abusers are facing great social and legal punishment for their sins. The beginnings of what has come to be called the Me Too Movement can be traced all the way back to 2006, but it was not until the hashtag campaign took off on social media in 2017 that it rose to widespread prominence, in conjunction with the publicized sexual-abuse allegations against Hollywood mogul Harvey Weinstein. Other celebrities and public figures encouraged people to share their own stories of abuse, assault, and victimization by powerful men. Certainly the movement did not eliminate abuse and mistreatment in the world, but the hope was that such actions would no longer be considered socially acceptable, since one of the main frustrations behind the Harvey Weinstein revelations (other than the abusive actions themselves) was the fact that so many knew about it and still said or did nothing.

The church for too long has been silent on abuse issues, even as stories of abuse have occurred *within* the church itself. The church must examine its own practices of patriarchy and confess, repent, and commit to doing better. The church must also create a healthy space for victims to share their stories as part of a space of lament and solidarity.

#BlackLivesMatter

Racial injustice has been even more divisive in the church and in the world than sexist injustice, and nowhere can the division be seen more clearly than in conversations about the Black Lives Matter Movement. Some would trace this movement's beginnings to the 2013 shooting of Trayvon Martin by George Zimmerman, but it did not gain much oxygen in the wider world until the 2014 deaths of Michael Brown in Missouri and Eric Garner in New York, both at the hands of police. Sadly, this movement's tender but angry rallying cry continued to play a role in the narrative of fatal interactions between United States police officers and the members of the black community in subsequent years, but it reached a fever pitch in the midst of the COVID-19 pandemic in 2020 following the killings of George Floyd in Minnesota and Breonna Taylor in Kentucky, among others.

At a very basic level, I hear the phrase "black lives matter" as a cry of lament from black women and men who can prove that, too often in the United States, the lives of people with darker skin have *not* mattered. We need only look at our country's shameful history of slavery, Jim Crow laws, segregation, mass incarceration, economic oppression, racial profiling, voter suppression, and on and on up to the present day to know their claim and their anger are valid. For too long the dominant culture in the United States has oppressed and suppressed and devalued black lives and black bodies.

Christians who believe in the gospel of Jesus Christ know that such maltreatment is sinful and has no place in the new creation kingdom of God. I and many of my white Christian sisters and brothers have been too complacent and often complicit in failing to hear or heed the cries, which means we have had a hand in exacerbating racism in the United States. The church must lament the past and present evils, but in our lament, we are also invited to confess our own sins and seek God's help in healing our land. Although being quiet and humble to listen and learn from the stories and pain of people of color in the United States is difficult and sometimes awkward, to do so also feels like a fresh wind of the Holy Spirit blowing in ways I can't recall happening previously in my lifetime. This movement does not feel like a spark of protest that will be extinguished quickly; rather, it feels like the beginning of a continental shift that, should we heed it, will help move us closer to love and equality for all.

It was disheartening when many became defensive or resistant to hearing the cry of lament about the stain of racism that has been present in the United States from the beginning. Some with power and influence have worked hard to sweep it under the rug, for fear that to really hear and deal with this issue would call for a deep change to the status quo. It was also disappointing when other movements arose not in solidarity but in opposition to the most recent iteration of the racial justice movement. Instead of acknowledging the particular struggle and version of empire oppression the black community has uniquely suffered in the United States, some sought to dilute the force of their message by claiming that "all lives matter" instead of "only" black lives. This response represented a distortion and misunderstanding of the message. Just as Jesus was willing to leave the ninety-nine to go and find the one lost sheep, we (those with power and privilege benefiting from empire allegiance) must have eyes to see and ears to hear, seeking out those who are especially hurting and in pain. God can be found in and among those in pain. Certainly, black lives are not the only lives currently in pain and peril. I have many brown friends who are struggling, many poor friends who are in despair. To care about the Black Lives Matter Movement does not mean we stop caring about other groups who need help. The call for the Christian church is to continue the ministry of Jesus Christ—to go to *all* those hurting and on the margins, and care for them. Our politics is one of compassion as part of the kingdom of God.

An important matter of clarification is that we must distinguish between the 501c3 official BLM organization and the racial justice movement represented by the hashtag campaign that began on social media. These are two different things, and the spirit of the movement is not embodied by those who started an official organization using the name of the movement, who then proceeded to misappropriate funds or promote non-Christian ideals. Every movement is going to attract opportunists and frauds who seek to capitalize on whatever issue has people's attention in a given moment. In fact, the New Testament affirms that even early Christianity was not immune to this phenomenon (see Acts 8:9–24). In the same vein, some have used the guise of the Black Lives Matter Movement to promote ideals or values Christians would not and should not affirm. Such perversion does not negate the importance of the movement itself, nor does it absolve Christians of our obligation to hear and respond to race-related lament in Christlike ways. I choose to identify as Christian despite a number of people who have said and done things under the banner of Christianity that I find abhorrent. It is important to understand that the root of the Black Lives Matter Movement is one of nonviolent resistance in the tradition of John Lewis and Martin Luther King, Jr. The waters of understanding have been muddied by the agitators who want to sow dissent and discord because that is how empire can flourish. But our black brothers and sisters are crying out in pain, and they need to be listened to, loved, and cared for.

In the end, Jesus cares for all people. He spent most of his time not simply *with* those on the margins from the civic and religious spheres of influence but also *as* one of those people. For the martyr church to faithfully be the body of the crucified and resurrected Christ, the church must be present in lament, advocacy, and solidarity with all who are beaten, bruised, and exploited, no matter the color of skin, gender, economic location, or any other identifying detail that puts them on the margin. The coming kingdom of God seeks the flourishing of life for all persons. The church must never settle for anything less.

Conclusion

As there is one Lord, one faith, one baptism (Ephesians 4:5), there is one church—the body of the crucified, resurrected, ascended Jesus Christ. The incarnation was the inauguration of new creation coming to earth as in heaven. The church is united with Jesus Christ in the power of the Spirit by the will of the Father to continue to be healed and renewed in Christ's image to participate in the kingdom that is here yet still coming.

The creeds testify and pray that the church is *one*—united in Jesus's love; *holy*—set apart to bear the image of the slaughtered lamb of God; *catholic*—inclusive of every tribe and nation; and *apostolic*—grounded in the crucified and resurrected Christ.

Jesus Christ is the model and means of the church's salvation that God desires to work in the world by the power of the Spirit. The church continues to live out its healing in Christ by participating in God's ongoing mission, which is justice and healing for all nations. While each individual person is invited to respond, God desires that humans navigate this healing and mission *together* with other humans. Togetherness is not easy. Christians do not always agree, but by the Spirit a greater unity can spring forth within bountiful diversity. The church is the bride of Christ. The church has failed in many ways and still needs to grow in maturity to better reflect God's image. The church has also been empowered by the Spirit to participate in the healing of all nations in amazing ways on this globe. God has been and will continue be faithful.

As the Spirit invites the church into greater days of faithfulness, the posture and methods of the church must resist the empire's seduction of power, control, and domination. The martyr church is invited to be set free from the power of fear, which often leads to violence. The church is invited to find life by taking up its cross in obedience for the sake of the kingdom. As God has *been* faithful, God will *be* faithful. Christian hope is not optimism or wishful thinking. The God who raised Jesus Christ from the dead has begun the healing of all creation, and God will see it unto completion (see Philippians 1:6). Although the evening news may cause us to lament and pray, our crucified and resurrected Savior invites us to hope. We are not afraid of death, but in joyful hope and compassion and love, we give our life back to God in thanksgiving.

God remains on the loose. Let all of us who have ears to hear and eyes to see offer ourselves to more fully be the body of the crucified and resurrected Christ for the glory of God!